Foster Child

A Midcentury Jewish American Boyhood

ISAAC KRAMNICK

Department of Near Eastern Studies & the
Program of Jewish Studies, Cornell University

Library of Congress Cataloging-in-Publication Data

Names: Kramnick, Isaac, author.
Title: Foster child : a midcentury Jewish American boyhood / Isaac Kramnick.
Other titles: Occasional publications of the Department of Near Eastern Studies and the Program of Jewish Studies, Cornell University ; v. 7.
Description: Produced for the Department of Near Eastern Studies & the Program of Jewish Studies, Cornell University, [2023] | Series: Occasional publications of the Department of Near Eastern Studies & the Program of Jewish Studies, Cornell University ; number 7 | Includes bibliographical references and index.
Summary: "An autobiographical account of the life of historian Isaac Kramnick and his upbringing as a foster child"— Provided by publisher.
Identifiers: LCCN 2022031005 | ISBN 9780578288598 (paperback)
Subjects: LCSH: Kramnick, Isaac—Childhood and youth. | Foster children—Massachusetts—Biography. | Jewish children—Massachusetts—Biography. | Foster home care—Massachusetts—History—20th century. | Millis (Mass. : Town)—Biography. | LCGFT: Autobiographies.
Classification: LCC HV883.M4 K73 2023 | DDC 362.73/3092 [B]—dc23/eng/20220721
LC record available at https://lccn.loc.gov/2022031005

Printed in the United States of America
Produced for the Department of Near Eastern Studies & the Program of Jewish Studies, Cornell University

10 9 8 7 6 5 4 3 2 1

This has been printed on acid-free paper. Publications on uncoated stock satisfy the minimum requirements of American National Standard for Information Sciences—Permanence of Paper for Printed Library Material, ANSI Z39.48–1992.

FOSTER CHILD

Occasional Publications of the Department
of Near Eastern Studies & the Program of
Jewish Studies, Cornell University

NUMBER 7

Edited by Ross Brann

*Publication made possible by gifts to the
Department of Near Eastern Studies &
the Program of Jewish Studies, Cornell
University*

*Sincere thanks to Patrick Alexander and his
colleagues at Penn State University Press for
their invaluable assistance in producing this
memoir*

*Dedicated with gratitude to the
Spiro and Mael families, to the
social workers, and to the teachers
who nurtured Isaac's early years.
And to his grandchildren—
Madeline, Anna, Sam, and Milo,
whom he helped nurture in his later
years with vast reservoirs of love.*

CONTENTS

The chorus of honking taxis and the chattering lunchtime legions walking with me up Fifth Avenue seemed to echo my exultant feelings that perfect spring weekday in 1975. Down from Ithaca, I was meeting Martin Kessler, my publisher at Basic Books, for the canonical lunch to celebrate turning over the completed manuscript of my book on Edmund Burke. It would be my second book, following the publication seven years earlier of my PhD dissertation on Lord Bolingbroke. A second book, I always tell my graduate students, is the marker of true distinction for academics. For if anyone says "I just read your book," you can ask "Which one?" whether you have written two or twenty.

As the midday crowds parted before my joyful steps, I sensed a small commotion halfway up the block. Ever the cautious country bumpkin in the big city, I tensed as I saw people walking around an overweight and disheveled beggar headed in my direction, whistling while jingling coins in a paper coffee cup. As he approached, I realized in shock that I recognized the man. He was my brother Leon, one of the hundreds of thousands of mentally ill people who had been deinstitutionalized in the early 1960s. Since then, Leon had led a peripatetic life as a vagrant and street person across the East Coast and the upper Midwest. We had met sporadically in the previous decade, usually at lunch counters in shabby big-city bus stations.

I cursed the coincidence of Leon panhandling on Fifth Avenue on this of all days, though I realized as he neared me that here on the sidewalk we were anonymous, and I could simply walk up, offer a greeting, and continue, less merrily, to be sure, to Fifty-Third Street and the office of Basic Books. In an instant I decided that he would not spoil my day. The merest interaction with him would take me back to painful thoughts of our family and childhood. I darted quickly into the doorway of Saks, and from inside the store

I watched him pass, the sweat rolling down his chubby smiling face
as someone gave him a coin. My prideful day had come to this, sidestepping to avoid my brother.

That extraordinary walk up Fifth Avenue haunted me for months
after the "publisher's lunch": the unabashed excitement in my success and the cowardly avoidance of the past that was the marker of
how far I had come. A scholar of history, I was managing far too
easily to avoid my own. Of course, I knew the broad outlines of my
story, fixed at least in memory from the age of five, but I visited
those years much less frequently than I did my eighteenth-century
scholarly texts.

Strengthened by a sense that my past could not hurt me, with
the tenure, books, happy marriage, and three children to prove it,
and moved by my guilt over dodging Leon, I decided to ask the
Commonwealth of Massachusetts for the records covering my childhood years in foster care. I knew one existed since a sympathetic
social worker had shown them to me in my college years. Three
years, scores of letters, and several helpful state administrators later,
I received in the mail in 1978 a hefty manila envelope, the story of
my life, just as I turned forty. I now had a text to study, Case No.
24269, a bureaucratic account of my boyhood years kept by initialed,
though otherwise anonymous, social workers of the Massachusetts
Division of Child Guardianship. There was no more sidestepping.

Here then is my story. It is a story about a certain time in the
American past, the early and middle twentieth century. It is a story
about one of the millions of families who made the monumental
move from the old country to an America whose streets would not
be paved with gold. This is a story of an American Jewish family,
two parents and three sons, that never realized the American dream,
unlike those chronicled by the great postwar Jewish novelists. The
fabled promise of America would elude all but one in this family,
the son who had darted into Saks that spring day in 1975.

CHAPTER 1

Sarah and Max

I never met my mother, who died when I was fourteen. Only when I was forty did I see my first photograph of her. When I was born in 1938, Sarah was a patient in a Massachusetts mental hospital. Since my father Max could not afford to raise me, I became a ward of the Commonwealth of Massachusetts when I was a month old, a "state kid," as I was labeled by my childhood chums.

Max, who I would see occasionally as I was growing up, was a slight, seemingly weightless, perpetually unhappy man. Born in 1885 in Grodno, a city in northwest Poland, then part of the Russian Empire, he was the second son of Esther and Israel Kramnick. A tailor in his shtetl, Israel had four sons, two of whom, Abraham and Max, would come to America. The other two, whose names are not in my records, perished along with their parents in the Holocaust. My Uncle Abraham, the elder brother, was a socialist agitator in Poland, who had from age sixteen distributed anti-tsarist broadsides in peasant villages at night, hiding during the day. Arrested, he escaped execution by agreeing to join the tsar's army. He jumped out of his troop train, and, according to relatives I would meet as an adult, he tramped across Europe with a broken ankle, landing finally in Liverpool, England, where he lived for five years before coming to New York in 1904, the first Kramnick in the new world. He lived on Clinton Street on the Lower East Side, and like so many other newly arrived Jewish immigrant men, Abraham worked in a sweatshop for the garment trade. He remained true to his socialist principles in the new world, spurning opportunities to own his own shop because he did not want to employ—and therefore exploit—workers.

Jews had lived in America since the colonial period, with some 1,300 in the thirteen states immediately after independence. By 1830, the year of Tocqueville's famous visit, there were 4,500 Jews in America. These numbers swelled in the first great wave of Jewish immigration to America, the arrival of several hundred thousand German Jews in the middle decades of the century, bringing the number of Jews in America to a quarter of a million by 1880. Some of the German Jews were liberals and intellectuals fleeing the failed revolutions of the midcentury, but most were petty traders and deal-ers settling in different cities throughout America, beginning their lives here as dry goods peddlers, sellers of clothing, furniture, and junk. A small fraction of these men would become owners of retail stores; an even smaller number would rise from peddler to depart-ment store owner, as in the fabled rags-to-riches lives of Adam Gimbel, Benjamin Bloomingdale, Edward Filene, A. L. Neiman and Herbert Marcus, Benjamin Altman, Nathan and Isidor Strauss (Macy's), and Julius Rosenwald (Sears, Roebuck & Company).

My uncle Abraham Kramnick was part of the next and larg-est wave of Jewish immigration to America, from Eastern Europe, mainly Poland and Russia, which in the forty years between 1880 and 1920 increased the number of Jews in the United States from 250,000 to 3,600,000. This vast diaspora was triggered by the assassination of Tsar Alexander II in 1881. Jews were falsely accused of the regi-cide, and officially sanctioned pogroms erupted in over two hundred cities and towns in the 1880s. Millions of Russian and Polish Jews, like Abraham, were exiled or fled west, escaping the anti-Semitic violence endemic in the vast Russian Empire. Over half a million of these Eastern European Jews lived in New York City when Abraham Kramnick settled in its Lower East Side. There were loud voices, of course, seeking to close America to my sort. Even as my mother and father's families arrived in America, Henry Cabot Lodge, who was the personification of the proud Yankee past of Massachusetts and who wrecked the League of Nations, urged the US Senate to keep non-Anglo-Saxon immigrants out of America.

More precious even than forms of government are the mental and moral qualities which make what we call our race. They are exposed to but a single danger, and that is by changing the quality of our race and citizenship through the wholesale infusion of races whose traditions and inheritances, whose thoughts and whose beliefs are wholly alien to ours and with whom we have never assimilated or even been associated in the past. The danger has begun. There lies the peril at the portals of our land; there is pressing in the tide of unrestricted immigration. The time has certainly come, if not to stop, at least to check, to sift, and to restrict those immigrants.

Such views were commonplace among Boston Brahmins. In 1907, three years after Abraham Kramnick arrived, Henry Adams—the descendant of two presidents, and a leading American historian and intellectual—published a small private edition of his autobiography for selected friends. When mass published posthumously in 1918, *The Education of Henry Adams* would win the Pulitzer Prize, and it was ranked first on the Modern Library's 1998 list of the twentieth century's one hundred best nonfiction books. It contained, though, a strikingly anti-Semitic passage, perhaps meant originally only for his close friends. The passage always seems to speak to me of my own origins, invoking, as it does, my name. To define himself, Adams enlisted an alien other. He was "not a Polish Jew fresh from Warsaw or Cracow, not a furtive Yacoob or Ysaac still reeking of the Ghetto, snarling a weird Yiddish to the officers of customs—but had a keener instinct, an intenser energy, and a freer hand than he—American of Americans, with heaven knew how many Puritans and patriots behind him."

Like so many recently arrived Polish Jews, Abraham sent money to bring his younger brother, Max, then twenty-one, to America. Max arrived in New York on January 30, 1906, on the *Noordam*, out of Rotterdam. He did not settle in New York but used more of Abraham's money to travel around the eastern United States. For some reason lost to my family's history, Max then decided to return to Poland. Abraham never forgave Max for this decision. He never wrote or spoke to his brother again, regarding him as a worthless ne'er-do-well.

Returned to Grodno, Max became a factory worker. Uneducated and uninterested in Judaism, he spent his time, as he would tell it, working and reading newspapers.

My mother, Sarah Sushelsky, was born in America, on January 19, 1893. Her parents had emigrated in 1890 from Janow (a city close to Grodno) to Fair Haven, Massachusetts, near New Bedford, where her father, Zusel, became a farmer and a Hebrew teacher. In Poland, Zusel had married his niece, Rachel Sushelsky, my grandmother, a blood transgression that many in the family see as the original sin that taints us all. His pictures show a stern round-faced man with sunken eyes and a full white beard. Grandfather Sushelsky took his family back to Poland in 1895 when my mother was two.

Until the success of Frank McCourt's *Angela's Ashes*, most people did not realize that many Irish and Italian immigrants returned to the old country. Jews virtually never did. Why go back to pogroms? Yet my maternal grandfather and my father did. I do not know why my bachelor father returned, but my grandfather went back, he told people, because Jews in America were not religious enough and because he discovered the streets were not paved with gold. A more likely reason is that when his father died in Poland, Zusel inherited a dye mill. He seems to have prospered for a while, but ultimately the enterprise failed. His wife died in 1916. Eight years later, in 1924, Zusel returned to America, leaving behind my mother, who had married in 1922. This time he became a Hebrew teacher in Lynn and Salem, Massachusetts, where two older children who had remained in America lived: a son, Bernard, who owned a grocery store, and a married daughter, Goldie. Zusel soon remarried and then divorced. Three years before he died in 1929, at the age of seventy-five, he and Bernard sent money so that my mother and her family could return to America.

Unlike my father, Sarah had had five years of schooling in Poland, enough to enable her to help in Zusel's business and get her a job in the library, where she met my newspaper-reading father. They married in 1922, when he was thirty-seven and she twenty-nine. Max had no work and Sarah's family took him into the business, which would soon fail. My older brother Leon was born in 1924. When the money arrived in 1926 to bring her family to America, Sarah could do so immediately because she was already an American citizen. Max and Leon, who were Russians, made the trip six months later.

Sarah went by train from Poland to France, where she was to take the steamer. But on the way to France she had a mental collapse and spent a month in a clinic outside Paris. Family lore has it that this incident came to light only after the French authorities sent the bill to my grandfather in Massachusetts. My mother's own account, recorded in a lucid moment and reported in her hospital file, was that "I felt very lonesome. I felt I didn't want to go to America. I was not sure I could stand it." Her crisis persisted after she was released and on the boat. Confined to her bunk in steerage for trying to jump overboard, she failed to recognize her sister, Goldie, from Salem, who met her when she arrived at Ellis Island. To make matters worse, she had lost her clothes in transit, other than what she wore, and when Max's brother Abraham bought her some, he told her she had married a worthless man who only read newspapers. Her depression subsided shortly after she arrived in Massachusetts, and the next three years were, apparently, the happiest of her married life.

The reconstituted family of three settled in the North Shore, near my mother's sister in Lynn and her father and brother in Salem. In their first six years in this country, Sarah and Max moved numerous times: from Beverly to Salem, back to Beverly, again to Salem, finally settling in Beverly in 1933. Some fifteen miles northeast of Boston, the small neighboring cities of Lynn, Salem, Beverly, Danvers, and Peabody were magnets attracting newly arrived Jewish, Greek, and Italian immigrants to their factories and mills. Dominating the region were the electronic plants in Lynn (in one of which Herbert Philbrick would later become an American Cold War hero for having "led three lives for the FBI") and the leather mills of Peabody, in which my father worked all his life. Peabody was then, in fact, one of the world's largest producers of leather, with nearly ninety tanneries employing over nine thousand workers. Accessible by trolley from Boston, about an hour away, Peabody, Beverly, and even Lynn and Salem still had some farmland, but for the most part the recent immigrants lived near the city centers in gritty collections of large three-story wooden houses, home often to six or eight families, or in the occasional larger wooden tenement like the one my parents lived in after 1933 in Beverly, which housed fifteen families.

Crowded and poor though they were, Sarah and Max in their first years in America lived what appeared to be the first chapter in the story of immigrant success. These were apparently happy years for my mother, who adored her Leon, her radio, and moving picture shows. Max seemed economically secure in the tanneries, read his newspapers at night, and continued to have nothing to do with communal Jewish life, much to the regret of his father-in-law. Hard times began in 1929 and 1930 with the sudden deterioration of Sarah's mental health. In the six years after Leon's birth she had had two miscarriages and one stillbirth. She complained of constant stomach pains and heart trouble, which Max dismissed as imaginary. Devastated by the death of her father in 1929, she became convinced that his absence freed her husband to treat her badly. Max and Sarah fought constantly. What she perceived as Max's sudden mistreatment coincided with the birth in 1930 of my brother Sigmund, whose arrival apparently produced fits of resentment and jealousy from six-year-old Leon, making life even more miserable in the cramped apartment.

While his family disintegrated around him, my father was caught up in the uncertainty of the Depression, which in Peabody was exacerbated at the leather mills by the popularity of DuPont's new leather substitutes. Max was active in the drive to unionize the leather workers, which led to a strike of 5,100 workers in Peabody when the manufacturers refused to recognize the union. When scabs arrived from Maine and New Hampshire, there were riots, tear gas, and arrests. While Max was unharmed, his work and earnings were sporadic.

Fig. 1 |
Sarah Sushelsky, Isaac's
biological mother

Fig. 2 |
Max Kramnick, Isaac's
biological father

My mother and father never found the promised land of opportunity in the United States, no streets paved with gold. America for
them in the 1930s was a land of pain, misery, and failure. Even as the
family received assistance from the Massachusetts Division of Aid
and Relief, Sarah began accusing Max of being disrespectful, cruel,
and abusive. In 1933 she brought Max to Salem court. He was put
on probation for assault and ordered to give Sarah $10 weekly from
his $18 on again, off again weekly paycheck, from which $5 went for
rent. The principal at Leon's school, Sarah told the judge, had said
that Max beat Leon because he had fought with baby Sigmund. With
the assistance of the Jewish Society for the Prevention of Cruelty to
Children and other benevolent societies, Sarah had Max removed
from home for extended periods, during which he made payments
to the family through the probation officer.

Sarah also turned on nine-year-old Leon, bringing him to the
Beverly Habit Clinic in December 1933, which concluded that Leon's
problems were, as his state file puts it, "jealousy, disobedience, indifference, destructiveness and lack of companions." Eight months
later she took Leon to court "on a complaint of stubbornness," and
Judge Sears found him "delinquent," ordering that the Massachusetts
Division of Child Guardianship place him in a foster home. He
was sent to live with a farm family in Norton, Massachusetts. Leon
was gone, but after two months, Sarah changed her mind and told
neighbors, police, and the court that the state had stolen him and
that she had agreed to his departure only because she thought he
was going on a summer vacation. Because of her repeated requests,
Leon was returned home in February 1935, despite evidence of Sarah's
own mental deterioration. Neighbors informed the police that she
sometimes slept all day and didn't feed the children. She, in turn,
complained to the police of neighbors plotting against her, and of
one in particular who wanted to kill her. To make matters worse,
in 1935 Max was laid off, and some of the furniture in their three-
room apartment was repossessed.

Meanwhile, Sarah demanded that the courts give her a divorce.
In addition to his physical abuse, Max, she claimed, was sleeping
with other women. Three times she used lawyers from the Boston
Legal Aid Society and social workers from Boston's West End Jewish

Family Welfare Society to argue that she be allowed to divorce Max and move to Boston with her two sons. Unsuccessful in getting a hearing the first two times, in February 1936 she was permitted to make her own case. In rambling, semicoherent English and Yiddish, Sarah put Max and his infidelity at the center of a plot involving neighbors, relatives, and officials, all bent on hurting and even killing her. Her case record attempts a summary of her courtroom comments.

On one occasion she went to the brother's home and brother was not home. During the visit she went out of the house for a few minutes and claimed when she came back she saw her husband and sister-in-law coming out of the bedroom together. She told her brother that his wife was unfaithful. Since that time brother has had nothing to do with her. She says that her husband has mistreated her, that he disconnected the wires in the radio to keep her from having pleasure, took the wheels off her son's bed, and did other things to make life very unpleasant for her. She says that he told her he is through with her. Besides these and other complaints concerning her husband, she says that another woman who lives in the same house calls her names and says she is crazy, and that the woman struck her in the chest and pushed her onto a couch, which made her left arm so sore that she went into the Massachusetts General Hospital for treatment. They told her to soak her arm in hot water, so she came home and was going to take a bath and left the boy in another room, telling him not to go out. She says that while she was in the bathroom she heard the woman ask the boy to go to her apartment and when he refused to, she took him and locked him in. She rushed out and threatened to break the door if the woman wouldn't let the boy out, so she did, and she took him into the bathroom while she finished her bath. She has called the police twice about this woman and her husband in the past few weeks. She claims that this woman pushed her onto a table and tried to kill her.

How much of her tirade Judge O'Brien understood is unclear, but he decided, rather than grant a divorce and require Max to give her money, to send Sarah to the state psychiatric hospital in nearby Danvers for ten days of observation, because "she talks too much" and is "incoherent." According to Sarah's case record, "She was taken there by two police officers and a police matron."

Judges, police, and public officials, in general, in 1930s Massachusetts had names like Sears and O'Brien, and it's interesting to speculate how much of my mother's difficult encounters with public institutions, agencies, and officialdom can be explained in part by the vast social, cultural, ethnic, and linguistic distance between her and "the system." There were no police or court interpreters and virtually no Jewish presence in officialdom whatsoever. In the 1930s, over 125,000 Jews lived in the greater Boston area, some 30,000 of them in the working-class cities north of Boston: Chelsea, Malden, Lynn, Salem, and Peabody. The latter, with a population in 1935 of almost 20,000 people, 1,200 of whom were Jewish, had but one Jewish official in this period, Elihu Hershanson, who served on the school committee and the City Council before he became the city solicitor. The one Jew involved in my mother's case, a Salem Jewish attorney, Philip Hurwitz, helped my father Max defend himself. The relevance of these reflections on the political-legal realities of immigrant group life in Depression-era Massachusetts to the official finding of talking too much, and too incoherently, recedes dramatically but never totally as she was clinically evaluated at Danvers State Hospital. The observation team notes:

Although it was often difficult to see the connection between her remarks and the question that had been asked, the relationship grew apparent as she continued. She was voluble and overproductive in conversation. She was quite unstable, became excited, easily or almost burst into tears on many occasions while discussing her domestic problems, but was usually calm and pleasant while telling of her early life. She was suspicious, irritable and resentful when talking of her family life and neighbors. She says that she feels very sad about not being with her children, because since she has felt that her husband no longer cares for her she has transferred all her affection to the two children. She has been on ward B-1 all during her stay here, has been quiet but tearful and frequently asked to go home. She has been cooperative, attentive, emotionally unstable, restless and rather irritable and resentful toward her husband. She said that she has had to have police protection because her husband and a neighbor woman have mistreated her. Her grasp of general information and knowledge of current events is fair, considering her language and educational handicaps.

She is reported to often mumble to herself in Yiddish, and "due to her accent and steady stream of talk when she does say anything it is rather difficult to understand everything this patient says." Who knows, then, to what extent her mumbling in a strange tongue influenced the clinical reading of her mental condition?

As part of their evaluation procedures, the hospital staff also examined police records and statements obtained from relatives, neighbors, and social service organizations, all of which were generally supportive of Max. Sarah's brother, Bernard Sushel, the grocer from Salem, for example, insisted that Max was a man of fine character and branded as delusions Sarah's claims of philandering. Her brother's wife added that Sarah was always untruthful and a troublemaker. Neighbors told police that Max was not the kind of man to have affairs with women friends and that Sarah was suspicious every time he chatted with a female. He went out on some evenings, they confirmed, but only to be free of her nagging and to forestall a fight. The only informant to criticize Max was the social worker who had handled Leon's entry into foster care in 1934, who wrote that Max exhibited a "sneering attitude" toward Sarah.

Neighbors and relatives described Sarah as having no interest in the apartment, spending most of her time in bed, and often borrowing food: "She was not a good manager and spent money foolishly. Her son admitted that she had asked him to go to court and testify a lot of lies against her father. Her sister-in-law says that patient was untruthful and a trouble-maker. She is said to have threatened to hit her husband with a chair." Their sense was that she quarreled constantly with her husband and on occasion threw his clothes into the street and ordered him to leave. Also weighing in against Sarah were some of the agencies that had previously helped her. The

Boston Legal Aid Society now wrote that she was "a pest and a nuisance . . . a beggar type of woman." The Beverly Hebrew Ladies Aid Society had discovered that she had three relatives who had been mentally ill and wanted to have nothing more to do with her.

At the end of the ten-day observation period the hospital authorities were divided. One doctor insisted that Sarah was not emotionally unstable, if perhaps a bit paranoid. He thought "the basis of this women's ideas are her husband's sexual indifference." Another wrote, "I don't see how we can commit her," while a third doctor felt, "We have enough to commit her on. Her ideas are paranoid and she is psychotic." In late March they reported to the judge that even though the evidence of mental disorder was not sufficient to warrant permanent commitment, Sarah should be kept at Danvers for further observation and only discharged if improved.

My father visited the Danvers State Hospital each week that February and March. He told the authorities that he wanted Sarah home, despite their constant fighting, because "he didn't know what to do with the two children, especially the little one who cried all the time for his mother." He convinced the Danvers staff to let my mother come home for a trial period in early April. The doctors agreed, moved perhaps by Sarah's repeated promises to forgive Max's indiscretions and by what she reported as her overwhelming need to be with her children.

Sarah's return was a disaster. Six-year-old Sigmund was living with a paternal cousin's family in Salem, and Sarah returned to a filthy apartment with a feuding Max and Leon. Stubborn, uncooperative, and large for his age, twelve-year-old Leon physically intimidated Max and Sarah, even as they resumed screaming at each other. The turmoil at home ended in September when complaints by neighbors that she was a nuisance in the tenement caused the chief of police to drive Sarah back to Danvers State Hospital.

As she returned to Danvers, Leon was returned the same month to foster care, once again to a farm, this time in West Medway, a town about thirty miles southwest of Boston. Leon's "bold and impudent" mistreatment of his parents and his mother's renewed absence from home led the Division of Child Guardianship to reactivate Judge Sears's order of 1934 that the "delinquent" be removed from home.

The Division's social worker who monitored his case described him as "a heavy, stolid type whose reactions are slow. Is lacking any sense of humor. Looks ready to cry when spoken to. He is an odd sort of boy, uncommunicative, lacking in force and not at all of the rough, happy-go-lucky type."

In West Medway, Leon was teased by the boys at his small rural school for being a "state kid." Despite his recent pummeling of Sarah and Max, Leon refused to fight back at school. "Even the first graders can slap him in the face without any retaliation," the social worker noted, with Leon claiming to be "a man of peace." With coaching from the visitor about defending himself, he began hitting back anyone who picked on him. Leon did very well in school, which left the social worker all the more puzzled about his personal and social habits:

He has absolutely no sense of personal responsibility. One of the younger boys in the home has to tie his necktie, comb his hair, and at times even wash his face. Goes about in a slack manner unless he is watched at all times. Has no desire to play games with other boys, even though he has little to do on the farm out-side of carrying a pail of water to the horses. There does seem to be some mental twist in this boy's makeup which causes him to be so untidy and which also causes his lack of interest in nor-mal things for a boy his age.

Meanwhile, my father, who had moved into the large Lynn apart-ment of Sarah's recently divorced sister, Goldie Wise, and her two children, requested another trial visit at home for Sarah. Hospital officials resisted at first and then relented in June 1937, allowing it only "against advice." It was another disaster, with constant yelling and fighting, Sarah turning on everyone in the crowded tenement, cursing and accusing many of them of having amorous designs on Max. Nonetheless, in their half of Goldie's apartment, with seven-year-old Sigmund still living with a cousin in Salem and thirteen-year-old Leon in a foster home, I was conceived, even as the chaos and Sarah's mental deterioration led to more confron-tations with the neighbors. On June 29, 1937, short of three weeks after her visit began, the police returned Sarah to Danvers State Hospital. In December, when she was six months pregnant, my mother was transferred to the Worcester State Hospital because Danvers had no maternity facilities. I was born there on March 6, 1938. Six weeks later, I was brought from Worcester to the Boston office of the Division of Child Guardianship; I became a ward of the Commonwealth of Massachusetts, or as my case record puts it with bureaucratic brevity: "4/20/38—Isaac rec'd. cause for acceptance: Mo. Insane, Fa. Unable to provide."

CHAPTER 2

Mrs. Milford, Mrs. Perricotte, and Mrs. Bell

I was named for my father's grandfather and for a son born to Sarah and Max in Poland who died at six weeks. How appropriate a name it was. Isaac, *yitzchak*, means laughter in Hebrew, because when the elderly biblical Sarah was told by an angel that she was to give birth, she laughed. Perhaps along with more fraught responses, Sarah Kramnick laughed when she discovered at age forty-four that she was pregnant from an utterly unsuccessful visit home with her fifty-two-year-old husband.

My first foster mother, Mrs. Julia Milford, who took in state babies under a year old, lived in Newton Center when I was placed with her in April 1938. Four months later she and her husband moved to Cambridge. For my keep she received $4.00 a week. The state paid this basic board rate and a scheduled set of costs for clothing and medical expenses. In turn the state sometimes asked the biological parents for a weekly payment if they had the means. The system flourished in the 1930s with families earning extra money in hard times by feeding another mouth. If it were an older child, families acquired an extra hand to do chores at home or on the farm. Leon, for example, had been placed on a farm in 1937, and his job was to bring water to the horses. Of course, economics was not the only reason people took in foster children; good hearts, altruism, and loneliness played their roles, as well.

The Commonwealth of Massachusetts and its Division of Child Guardianship would play a crucially supportive role in my child-hood, responsible in part for my making it. I was lucky to be its beneficiary in an age when social welfare agencies were not yet overrun with at-risk clients and were still applauded for their good work. Massachusetts had the oldest foster care system in the United States, one acknowledged to be the leader among the then forty-eight American states in formulating and developing methods of public care for needy children. Its experience in this field began with the devastating impact of the Civil War on the families of soldiers. From 1863 to 1919 the State Board of Charities had within it a "Division of Minor Wards," which had developed an extensive network of private home placement offering foster care to "neglected," "depen-dent," or "delinquent" children, and children of "insane parents." Massachusetts introduced board payments to foster families and payment for public school education, which was fifty cents a week in 1896 when it was introduced. Even more enlightened was the 1879 requirement that a professional corps of "friendly visitors" monitor the well-being of each state ward.

In 1919, and very much a manifestation of the Progressive movement's professionalization of social services for the poor, Massachusetts re-created these bodies as the Department of Public Welfare and the Division of Child Guardianship, requiring civil ser-vice exams and adequate educational training for social workers in the foster care system. When I entered the system in the late 1930s, the Division of Child Guardianship, located in the basement of Boston's State House, had custody of some eight thousand children, most classified as "neglected" or "dependent" and about three hun-dred as "delinquent." All were placed in homes within forty miles of Boston, the maximum distance the Division assumed one of its visitors could travel in a day. Children under three in foster homes were supposed to be visited monthly, and every three months if older. In these visits the social worker was required to have a private interview with the child and call at the school he or she attended. In recording these visits Massachusetts law required notations on the health, food, clothing, and sleeping arrangements in the home, as well as "the duties and pleasures" of the child and his or her general development, sense of responsibility, and acceptance by the community. At the school the visitor was to ascertain the child's scholarship, attendance, and conduct, as well as the school's sense of the care the child was receiving at home.

With a budget in 1938 of two and a half million dollars, the state's care of foster children was enlightened. Educated social workers investigated prospective foster families, visiting their homes, even interviewing neighbors and soliciting character references. Printed brochures of instructions were sent to all foster mothers covering the quality of care and family life the home was expected to provide, including food, clothing, sleeping arrangements, assignment of household duties, school and church attendance, savings, and terms of board. Foster parents were informed they could not inflict corporal punishment "without the visitors' permission," and they had to provide periodic physical examination of all children under care. These laudable professional standards, which I have resurrected from historical archives, were surely not always practiced, especially since the supervision and surveillance provided by visitors had to be variable, since some had caseloads of nearly one hundred children. And even in 1938 remnants of more primitive assumptions about children and childhood were still at work. The visitor's "face sheet" in the file of each child they supervised, for example, had two columns to be filled out at each visit (see page 20). All this notwithstanding, and, even with the possibility of neglect or abuse, my experience with the Division of Child Guardianship and its visitors was a textbook case of successful social service. The Commonwealth of Massachusetts was concerned, supportive, nurturing, and encouraging. I was lucky.

I suppose I should consider myself lucky, as well, to have, unlike most adults, precisely detailed information about my infancy

CHARACTERISTICS	1	2	3	4	5
Affectionate					
Obedient					
Unselfish					
Truthful					
Honest					
Clean Minded					

APPARENT MENTAL CONDITION	1	2	3	4	5
Above Average					
Average					
Dull					
Backward					
Feeble Minded					
Idiotic					

preserved in meticulous visitor's notes in my file, my anonymously written biography, which I acquired when I was forty. It seems I slept through the night, from 11 pm to 6 am, at seven weeks old, which may explain why Mrs. Milford, according to the visitor, "considers him a nice baby." The visitor did, indeed, see me monthly, as required, first at Newton and then at Cambridge, recording each time, "Is a good natured child . . . a bright looking child. Coming along nicely . . . quite active . . . . Is a bright active little fellow . . . . Very affectionate."

When I was a year old in the spring of 1939, I was moved to the home of Mrs. Mildred Perricotte in Brighton. Two other foster children lived in the family, both under three, which, it turns out, was Mrs. Perricotte's specialty. In all my homes foster care seems to have meant life with a foster mother. The state's formal contract and placement was always with a "Mrs. So and So," married, to be sure, but the husband, the foster father, is invisible. Foster care provided an independent economic existence for some married women. Away at work, seldom at home for home visits, fathers are rarely present

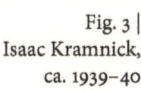
Fig. 3 |
Isaac Kramnick,
ca. 1939–40

in my case record or in my memory. My foster mothers also seem
to have been unusually strong minded and nurturing, which further eclipses any sense of father figures in my childhood. They were
there, of course, as is clear from the visitor's reference to a picture in
the Boston Globe of August 24, 1940, with me on top of the shoul-
ders of Mr. Perricotte in a crowd greeting President Roosevelt on
a campaign visit to Boston. But my biographical file, case #24269,
describes me thriving in this placement because of the capable care
of Mildred Perricotte. How unsettling for me as an adult to read of
myself and an unremembered foster mother, and to note the state's
concern that my "apparent mental condition" not be in the bottom
categories.

> Ch is doing beautifully in every way. A real fat, brown, nice
> boy . . . . Fos mo. rpts he is a real nice little boy now . . . .Is a
> very nice little ch., quite good looking . . . . Talks quite well for
> his age. Fos mo. v. fond of him . . . .V. good natured ch . . . .Ch.

learns v. quickly . . . he is full of life . . . is talking real plainly for his age. Also a smart little fellow . . . . A v. smart little boy . . . child appears to be a lovely normal kind of boy . . . is v. active and alert . . . .Fo. mo. very fond of this child . . . . Is apparently very happy . . . plays well with other children. child is very affectionate. Likeable child.

I seem, thankfully, not to have been perfect or totally unaffected by my situation. I cried to get my own way, even unto lying on the floor and throwing temper tantrums. I had trouble sleeping at night and would wake others by shaking my crib. "He has ruined one crib and fos. mo. says he will ruin the new crib shortly." I was "v. sensitive, particularly to noises. Fos. mo. rpts that even the birds singing frightens the ch." When Mrs. Perricotte told Max about this during one of his visits, "Fa. said he expected it, due to mo's condition when she was carrying ch."

Max visited me about every two months, which was his right, if he had cleared the time and date with both the Division of Child Guardianship and the foster home. On some occasions he brought Sigmund and even Leon, for in April 1939, buoyed by steady work and claiming he missed his son, Max's request that Leon be brought back from his foster home in West Medway to live with him was granted. Max, who had been pleased with Mrs. Milford's care, constantly found fault with Mrs. Perricotte over my appearance, my health, and what he felt was the disorganization of her household. In one diatribe Max declared that he "hated the state." My foster mother, in turn, reported that Max "was always complaining about her." The social workers tended to support Mrs. Perricotte, while assuring her that Max "was never satisfied with anything the State had done for Isaac." Thus began a fundamental feature of my life in foster care, a three-way tug of war over me between my biological father, my then foster mother, and the Commonwealth of Massachusetts.

My father's visits invariably upset Mrs. Perricotte. She told the state that he often violated the Division's rules, rules that parents of her two other state children followed. He showed up sometimes without the permit obtained from the Division's Boston office, which required prior notification of the foster mother; moreover, she complained, he often stayed longer than the hour limit per visit.

My father, it seems, brought me chocolates on his visits, although my foster mother forbade it. When she wasn't looking, he snuck the candy into my hand, I the willing accomplice. Claiming the chocolate made me sick, Mrs. Perricotte decreed that Max could not visit again if he brought candy. He was undeterred. On his next visit, when I had been dressed up especially nicely by her to go for a walk with Max, I got my clothes covered with chocolate, and mayhem ensued. These chocolate wars couldn't have been much fun for me, despite the instant pleasure, caught as I was between two strong wills.

Then came the "clothing crisis." On one of his visits Max brought a bundle of Sigmund's old clothes for me. Since they were far too big, Mrs. Perricotte insisted he take them back and give them to someone else who could use them. Max announced that "he wasn't giving anything to anybody for nothing." The social worker again sided with my foster mother, advising her to return the clothes to Max on his next visit. A month later, Mrs. Perricotte told Max that she didn't want the clothes because I would not be living with her after I was three and she didn't want the responsibility of keeping them. Max took back the bundle and in retaliation stuffed my pocket with candy.

In 1940, Max, sixteen-year-old Leon, and ten-year-old Sigmund were living with my mother's sister Goldie, in Lynn, in a triple-decker house with six apartments. Goldie and her two children, Sid and Roz, had two rooms, as did Max and my brothers, and they shared the kitchen. Many years later my cousin Roz would write:

I was 12 in 1940. Max was there and Ziggy and I do remember Leon. I think Leon was in high school. I remember that even at my young age, I observed that Leon's personal hygiene left a lot to be desired, and I especially remember his teeth which I thought never got brushed and had a greenish film. I also thought he was strange although I never knew why at that time. I can still picture Max sitting at the kitchen table with newspapers spread out all over the table, to read and to absorb herring juices. I do remember that he enjoyed "shmaltz" herring and boiled potatoes.

No sooner had Leon returned home than he and Max resumed their embattled relationship. Their noisy altercations made it impossible for them to continue sharing Goldie's apartment, so my father and two brothers moved in 1941 to their own apartment in another wooden triple-decker on Little's Lane, Peabody. Max, who had moved so many times in his first fifteen years in America, would remain in Little's Lane for the rest of his life.

The age of three was an important threshold in the foster care system. Infant care through temporary "baby farming" was replaced by more carefully planned long-term child placement. Before it took that step, the state asked Max if he wanted to take care of me. Max demurred. He could not provide for me but much preferred to have me taken care of by a relative rather than in another state home. No relative appeared, so in May 1941, when I was three years and two months old, I left Mrs. Perricotte, who, according to the social worker, had grown "particularly fond" of me in the two years she mothered me.

When he had handed me over to the state, Max, the unobservant Jew, had surprisingly signed a form asking that I be raised in the Jewish faith and in a Jewish home. Recognizing that I was probably in its care for the long haul, the state now made good on this request. I was placed with Mrs. Theresa Bell (not a very Jewish-sounding name, to be sure) in Malden, which, like neighboring Chelsea, was a small city north of Boston with a large Jewish community. With her husband and three children of their own, Mrs. Bell had for years augmented the family's income by taking in a state child. A young, intelligent, and kind woman with middle-class aspirations, Mrs. Bell needed money to take her children to the country for several weeks in the summer, and she wanted to own her own house. Mr. Bell was not interested in his own children, let alone a foster child. His gambling added to the family's economic difficulties, while his constant criticism of his wife led to nasty fights. None of these family tensions was helped by their eight-year-old daughter—a saucy, problem child—nor by the frequent presence of Mrs. Bell's mother, who lived nearby and often joined her son-in-law in criticizing her daughter.

I slept alone in a crib in what the social workers describe as "a large, pleasant and airy room," which I shared with Mrs. Bell's two sons. I talked often at first about "my sister Carolyn" and a "big brother," both from the Perricotte family. My new foster mother seems to have been impressed by my "clean habits" and my "perfect table manners." She told the social workers that I ate well, "was remarkably bright," and "gave her no trouble." In time she grew to like me, with the state visitors noting that she was devoted to me, and even suggesting I was "her favorite." I was, she told them, "the dearest child" she'd ever had from the state. It seems that I, in turn, became devoted to her, following her everywhere and developing with her what the social worker described as "an intense emotional bond." This with a woman of whom I have no memories whatsoever.

Max visited me about every two months and was much less critical of Mrs. Bell than of Mrs. Perricotte. Perhaps it was because his life had once again taken a dramatic turn in 1941 when troubles with Leon intensified. Leon tried to finish Peabody High School, but he was surly and disrespectful to the teachers, just as he was stubborn and disobedient at home. Max considered sending him to a Civilian Conservation Corps camp or to work in a leather mill but rejected both ideas, he told school authorities, because Leon was "too damn dumb."

Leon's only peace was found in the library or in a music shop listening to classical records. He became reclusive and unkempt; his hair was filthy, long, and uncombed. He talked and laughed to himself, referring incessantly to germs in his body and to dying or being dead. Sometimes he sat in his room and sang or drummed the table so loudly that the neighbors on Little's Lane called the police. In early January 1942, when he was nearly eighteen, he came down with the mumps and was taken, dirty and fearful, to the Board of Health Hospital in Salem. Two days later he tried to jump out the ward window and was strapped to the bed. Against Max's wishes Leon was taken by the Salem police with temporary care papers to Danvers State Hospital for observation. His admission note reads:

When seen at the time of admission this patient appeared to be markedly undernourished and weak. He spoke in an irrelevant and incoherent manner. Before answering any questions he wanted to know if there was a lie detector in the room. When assured that there was not he answered questions willingly and promptly but his answers were, at times, incoherent and irrelevant. He said at one time "they think I have a mental disease." When asked who "they" were he replied the people in the contagious hospital. This was so because they slipped him a dose of nicotine and this probably aggravated his mental condition. He makes numerous bizarre motions with his hands.

He thought that he was dead or dying depending on when the question was put to him. He thought a doctor was up on the ceiling looking down and talking to him. When he expressed the idea that he was dead he would relax on his back with his extremities spread out in a manner which he thought was that of a dead person. Whe he expressed the idea that he was dying he was afraid of anyone who came near him because he thought they were going to complete the job of putting him to death.

DIAGNOSTIC IMPRESSION: here we have a young adult white male with a definite hereditary taint and a very poor environmental background. It would seem that with this poor endowment constitutionally and the poor environment that mental illness in this patient was inevitable. He showed a reaction in which he was retarded, blocked, incoherent, irrelevant, hallucinated and deluded, manneristic and at times negativistic. He has been markedly withdrawn, seclusive, careless of his appearance, inactive and underproductive. The examiner feels that it is a classical picture of schizophrenia of the catatonic type and wishes to offer that diagnosis provisionally.

ETIOLOGY: hereditary taint and constitutional predisposition, perhaps a very poor environmental background.

RECOMMENDATION: continued hospital care and maybe considered for electro-shock therapy.

It was by no means clear how long my seventeen-year-old brother would be kept at the Danvers State Hospital, but it was becoming increasingly apparent in these same years that my mother, still at Danvers, was facing a long commitment. Entries in her hospital file provide vivid evidence of her decline:

Her conversation appeared somewhat incoherent although there was such a language difficulty that it is impossible to judge this accurately. However, she was very talkative and rambling. She says that her sister followed her every second, never left her alone. She hears her sister talking about her, says her sister is trying to take away her will. In addition to this she hears a lot of other voices and rambles on something about 50 years in prison.

She states that her sister is a prostitute who has protection from a governor and who has constantly been abusing her throughout all the many years she has spent in institutions. That it was through her sister that she came into the hospital. She states she frequently hears her sister talk, she hears of the crimes that her sister commits, which is mostly the murder of children. In addition to this she states that she can frequently see her sister running around the street in pink pajamas, luring men to the place where she lives. In addition to this she states that her sister keeps patient's husband locked in the apartment, giving him poor food to eat while she eats the very best.

She accuses the staff of obscene activities. She appears to be hallucinated constantly and all of her hallucinations center about her sister. On the ward she has been seclusive, mingling little with the other patients.

Also seen speaking to herself in Yiddish.

Steals and wears other patient's clothing and hoards all lost articles. Frequently gives herself enemas on every occasion that is possible.

Wore many articles of clothing including a towel. Stocking stuffed with wax paper which patient likes to have on hand in a clean condition with which to wipe her hands. Facial grimaces and entire lack of modesty. Talked continually in a confused manner about buying meat, her diet, the Mass. General Hospital, her husband, her sister, voices in the clouds, and the Danvers Hospital. Silly expression and smile even when talking about her sister trying to harm her. Wanted to kiss the examiner and display and handle genitals.

Patient became very assertive and threatening to nurse this morning in cafeteria. Threatened to throw a cup at nurse in cafeteria and said she was going to knock another nurse's head off. When she returned to ward she told another nurse that the reason she disliked one of the nurses was because she had her baby and would not give it to her. Became upset again in the lavatory and expectorated in another patient's face.

No surprise then, that Max was informed in 1941 "that during her stay at the hospital she has shown progressive evidence of mental regression and is not making a very satisfactory adjustment. The outcome is unfavorable for recovery, and she will probably have to be in the hospital indefinitely."

Shortly after Leon's hospitalization, the Division of Child Guardianship, concerned about a hereditary taint, ordered a mental examination for me at the Boston Psychopathic Hospital. Max was indignant, but, accompanied by a social worker and Mrs. Bell, I took the test in Boston and seemed to have passed with flying colors. The state was pleased; I was normal, with a good IQ and a mental age substantially above my biological age. The case entry concludes, "Isaac is a lovely, attractive boy, interesting, intelligent and appealing."

The state's expectations for a long placement with Mrs. Bell and any possibility I had for deepening my emotional connection with her were dashed shortly after I turned five. My foster mother unexpectedly asked the state in the spring of 1943 to look for a new home for me. Mr. Bell did not earn enough money to run the house, she reported. Already working Mondays and Fridays at Boston's Filene's Department Store while her own children were at school (and on those days paying someone a dollar to look after me), she realized she needed a full-time job.

By the time the Division's visitor came to the house to talk things over, Mrs. Bell had changed her mind. She had left Filene's and now worked daily from 3 to 11 pm at South Boston's Navy Yard, alongside hundreds of other women mobilized to build America's wartime arsenal. She hoped that she and her husband could manage with me when I started school the next year. She even suggested she might give up her night job. The social worker was skeptical, noting "the serious friction at home" and complicated work arrangements. While the husband returns at four and looks out for the children, "he is not interested even in his own children . . . and is a difficult person to live with, constantly critical of his wife." The caseworker indicated he was "searching to get this child placement in a good Jewish home" but so far had been unsuccessful. The poignancy of reading my file is intensified by finding out about this terribly painful episode of which I have absolutely no memory, perhaps because it was so painful to know at five and a half years old that I might be taken away from this foster mother to whom I had become so attached. The social worker describes a visit in August 1943, in the midst of all this uncertainty:

> Fos. mo. is devoted to child and makes much of him. Saw I. A tall, slender nice looking boy. Well shaped head, beautiful brown eye.
> I. very shy today. Crying much. This is unusual as heretofore he has been very friendly with visr. Visr. feels that this child hears himself discussed between fos. parents. Visr. advised fos. mo. that plans will have to be made for the removal of I. Fos. mo. pleaded that nothing be done at present.

Contributing to Mrs. Bell's ambivalence about keeping me must have been my fragile health. Among the very few letters I would find years later among Max's things after his death was one from her reporting that she had used up the money Max had left for extra milk and asking for another $1.00 a week for this purpose. "Isaac has been sick and even now has a bad cold. He can't gain weight when he burns up with fever. When his tonsils are taken out I hope in the fall, I expect to see an improvement. In the meantime I'll try to build him up here." She had no such trouble with her other children, she acknowledged, but if I didn't improve after my tonsils were out, she warned, "I'll give up trying, as much as I love him."

Fig. 4 | Leon Kramnick, Isaac's oldest brother

Meanwhile, the Division again approached Max. When Leon was committed to Danvers in early 1942 and no longer living at home, they asked Max to pay $6.00 of his weekly wages of $28.00 toward my upkeep; the board payments to Mrs. Bell were $4.00 a week and he agreed to pay only that amount. Now in 1943, when his weekly pay at Samuel Tarlow's leather mill had jumped to $40.00, the state asked Max to take me home. Conceding that he was doing well, my father declined, insisting he could not raise me since "there was no woman at home to take care of me." If Mrs. Bell was not working out, why not send me back to Mrs. Perricotte, he suggested, having forgotten how critical he had been of her.

In the fall of 1943, even though my foster mother had given up her job in the Navy Yard, Mr. Bell insisted I be taken from their home. He resented the small amount of board he received from the Division and saw no reason "why he should support a state kid." On the last state visit to the Bells on October 26 the social worker wrote, "Boy is much more friendly and less shy today as he believes that Vis. has given up the idea of removing him from this home. Boy is devoted to fos mo . . . she is truly interested in this boy and devoted to him.

There is a real bond between fos mo and I. Fos mo asked Vis. to be sure that I. gets a good home as he deserves anything that can be done for him."

I totally misread what was happening that day. The state removed me from the Bells on November 16. I never saw Mrs. Bell again.

I have no memories of her, nor, less surprisingly, of the two foster mothers who preceded her, no memories of being with them or taken from them, which means I did not consciously brood over any hurt from serial abandonments. Until I learned about them in detail when I was forty, from the files sent to me by mail from the state, I never felt burdened by the hell that was my early life, or if I did, I repressed it. Repression and denial, when they work, can be effective coping mechanisms, the backbone of resiliency.

Learning about my first five and a half years when I was forty produced neither rage nor resentment, no explosion of decades-long pent-up pain. But it did evoke an unsettling, quasi-metaphysical encounter with a me outside myself. It was almost as if, in a play on Descartes's famous insight, because I was the subject of a case-biography, I existed before any memories that I existed. The I who existed for that five and a half years, however, is a person from whom I remain disconnected. The repression continues, which makes this chapter in my life more biography than autobiography. The story I tell here, with its distanced tone, could just as easily have been written by someone else, and in a sense it was, based as it is on my file, not my memory or constantly reinforced family tales. I am not, of course, unscarred by these early years. I worry excessively about loss and separation. My dreams to this day involve infinite variations on themes of abandonment. I have what even for academics is probably too great a need to be noticed and admired. I am very short on trust, assuming most people ultimately let you down or desert you.

But in November 1943 my luck was changing. I hit the foster care jackpot, a permanent placement that would take me to young adulthood. My fourth foster home was the "good Jewish home" that succeeded far more than the well-intentioned but weary social workers of the Commonwealth of Massachusetts could ever have imagined.

CHAPTER 3

Millis

My new placement was "in the country." Only twenty miles from Boston, straight out State Route 109, Millis, settled in 1657 and incorporated in 1885, is on the west bank of the Charles River. It was a small town in rural America in the 1940s, with its principal streets named Main, Village, Plain, and Pleasant. No late nineteenth- or early twentieth-century three-decker wooden houses built for immigrant mill workers here. Single-family houses were clustered close together for about a half mile on all sides of the town center, while their density declined dramatically as isolated homes and hilly pasturelands took over on the edges of town. Named after a nineteenth-century notable, Lansing Millis, the town's meager historical landmarks were a 1714 Congregational church on the town common and the Dinglehole, a pit, formerly filled with water, where, legend has it, Puritans heard the ringing of the bell summoning witches to their evil rites and where on moonlit nights a headless man kept vigil. Life in wartime Millis was much duller.

The two thousand people who lived in Millis were mainly small farmers with some workers in the three local industries, Herman

Shoe, Ruberoid Roofing, and Cliquot Club Ginger Ale, which clustered about a mile from the town center. A few Yankee gentry owned estates on the edge of town, among whom Christian Herter, governor of Massachusetts and the future Eisenhower secretary of state, was the most well known. But Millis had nowhere as many Brahmins as neighboring Dover, where Saltonstalls and Cabots lived. So many of Dover's young people went to private school that the town had no public school. Less privileged Protestants, "swamp Yankees" in the local vernacular, made up the bulk of those who lived in Millis, along with a handful of Catholics and Jews and a number of Armenians.

The heart of town was the intersection of Main Street (Route 109) and Exchange Street, with stores running up each street about a quarter of a mile from the intersection. Exchange Street's business ran up to the train station, long ago converted into the police station. On Main Street stood the Millis Consolidated School, one large brick building in which all 250 of Millis's school-age children (and some from Dover) spent the years from kindergarten through twelfth grade. The town, radiating out about five or six miles from this center, was governed by three elected selectmen, with the annual town meeting held in the school auditorium, to which, indeed, anyone in town could come—and most adults did.

A real feeling of community existed here, for with few exceptions people who lived in Millis worked in town. Virtually no one commuted to Boston or surrounding towns in the 1940s before Route 128, the circumferential highway around Boston, was built. Civic pride flourished, grounded in a firm sense of place. Nearly half the town showed up at the high school graduation and for home football games. To be sure, one had to go to Medway, the nearby town where several years earlier Leon had been in a foster home, or Milford (further out Route 109) to see a movie or buy clothes, but very few townspeople missed the Memorial Day parade down Main Street, and everyone eagerly anticipated finding out who would recite "In Flanders Fields" when the parade reached the bandstand. Just as crowded was the annual summer "field days," with its traveling carnival complete with Ferris wheel and games of chance.

But my Millis was light-years removed from this almost bucolic expression of American small-town life. My Millis was more like

a Sholom Aleichem Eastern European Jewish shtetl than Norman
Rockwell Middle America. My new foster family was one of some
fifty close-knit Jewish families, most of whom lived on Village Street
about three miles from the center of town.

There had been Jews in Millis since early in the century. Most
had come at first by trolley from Boston, to peddle junk and dry
goods (clothes and kitchen ware), and then, discovering they liked
the country, many settled there on small farms, raising chickens and
some cows. It was a Jewish community utterly unlike any that Jewish
American writers were soon to vividly imprint on the American
imagination of the 1950s and 1960s. For starters, Millis's Jews were
Republicans during the New Deal. Although the Democratic Party,
for the first time in American politics, defended the rights of workers, winning the loyalty of millions of city immigrants and forging
an enduring love affair between ethnic Americans and FDR, Millis's
Jews, small-time farmers, had no need for New Deal social policies
or its support of unions. FDR was no hero here. Also, unlike their
urban cousins, Millis's Jews were generally anti-intellectual; they
didn't send their children to college and kept few books, other than
prayer books, in their houses. They worshipped in one of two small
wood-framed synagogues, or *shuls*, as we called them in Yiddish.
Members of one "wouldn't step a foot" into the other, since one was
for the more religious, the other for the less observant. Neither shul
was big enough to support a rabbi, but in Jewish worship none was
needed; any member of the *minyan* of ten men can preside over
religious services.

Four small summer hotels, Cohen's, Delnick's, Nathanson's, and
Novick's, tucked in among the houses, fields, and woods off Village
Street, gave this part of Millis a particular Jewish flavor and a small
place in Jewish-American social history. This was "the country,"
after all, and Jews from Boston, Chelsea, Everett, and Malden had
for decades spent summer weeks or the fall High Holidays in this
rural Jewish enclave seeking a *bisl luft*, a little air. What had begun
as boarding houses became by World War II small bungalow hotels,
each putting up perhaps one hundred people. The vacationers came
from the city first by trolley, then by bus, and eventually in their own
cars. These rather plain, unglamorous Jewish hotels never had the

space or the entrepreneurial savvy to become resorts. There wasn't much to do there. They boasted no recreational directors (tummlers), no swimming pools, no Milton Berles or Buddy Hacketts or Eydie Gormés, all of which could be found in their Catskill counterparts attracting New York City Jews by offering movies, good food, and pleasant walks. The clientele tended to be not-very-well-to-do elderly Jews who were satisfied with the country air and two shuls in walking distance. Even they stopped coming by the late 1950s, as the postwar economic boom made possible more upscale and multiseasonal vacations, first the Catskills or Miami Beach, then Arizona and beyond, and then the world. But when I grew up the hotels loomed in my small-town sensibilities as symbols of sophistication and sin.

The Jews of Millis kept to their own kind and had an ample share of colorful characters. The *shochet*, the ritual slaughterer, Mr. Wolpert, lived across the street from Delnick's Hotel. Loud and combative, he was ubiquitous in our section of town, with his bearded, *yarmulka*-topped head and blood-stained apron, busily berating a "summer Jew" who passed by the barn where he did his religiously prescribed killing. The butcher, Nussy Rosenfeld, lived near Novick's Hotel: a quiet man, tall and lean, who all year long sold meat from a small shed near his house. Morris Muchnick was a different sort, a farmer with enormous strength, who sometimes crossed into the *goyische* world as, of all things, a part-time town policeman. During Prohibition he accompanied federal agents in hot pursuit of alcohol still reportedly hidden away behind Delnick's Hotel. Lore has it that during the raid he overheard Mrs. Delnick tell her son in Yiddish to flee into the woods. Able to understand her, Muchnick dutifully turned the moonshiner in; so much for ethnic solidarity. But few of Millis's Jews were as distinctive as Joseph Mael, the bearded, fervently pious patriarch of the "good Jewish family" that was my new foster home. I very soon came to see him as my *zayde* (grandfather), proof enough of the state's success in placing me in his daughter's house.

In his late sixties when I came to Millis, my *zayde* was tall and ramrod straight, dignified and almost charismatic, his sharp eyes staring intently above his well-trimmed, round, white beard. Born in Poland, he, like many Jews, had been pressed into the tsar's army during the Russo-Japanese war, from which he deserted in 1904. With his wife and two small sons he made his way across Europe to Liverpool, England, and booked passage to America for $14.00. He and his wife Etta, a tiny, quiet, and frail foil to his imposing presence, settled on Village Street in Medway, just beyond the Millis town line, near Etta's brother, George Steinberg, who was a "customer peddler," selling jewelry, shirts, and dresses. Joseph Mael got a job sorting cloth for a tailor, working from seven in the morning until eleven at night for $1.25 a week. After moving up Village Street to Millis in 1917, he carried on a junk business for many years, buying anything—beds, old clothes, scrap metal—often from gentry families in neighboring towns and selling it to immigrant factory workers in Millis and Medway.

When I arrived in 1943, Zayde was in the chicken business with his son Eddy Mael and my foster father, Saul Spiro. He and my *bubby* (grandmother) lived in a simple two-story farmhouse separated, at some distance, from the street not by a lawn but by a small, hilly field. Behind the house was the small barn where chicks bought from other farmers were fed, fattened, and then sold to slaughterers. It was not a very lucrative business, with its profit, the marginal increment between purchase and sale price, dependent on the vagaries of the daily market.

Zayde Mael was not learned, nor intellectually inclined; he was a rigidly observant Jew on whose head I always saw either a hat or a *yarmulka*. His piety, his *frumkeit*, was central to his being. His religious old-world bearing, complete with his dogged insistence on speaking only Yiddish, made him an exotic, prophetic presence in swamp-Yankee Millis. He built his own synagogue in a field adjacent to his house, a square wooden building, no larger than his home. Formally called the Beth Jacob Synagogue, it was known by everyone in town as the Mael shul.

In Poland Joseph Mael had been orphaned at the age of nine, and before being forced into soldiery he had come under the wing of a pious *rebbe*, who in the European Hasidic tradition did much more than officiate at synagogue services. Central figures in shtetl life as teachers, adjudicators of disputes, and dispensers of kindly and stern pastoral advice, Hasidic rebbes spent most of their time studying, or "learning," poring over talmudic tomes, as their fathers and grandfathers had before them. Their followers, inherited along with the title of Rebbe, supported them, since the Rebbe's unremunerated work was learning, deciding, or advising.

In America my new zayde found his Rebbe in the Dorchester section of Boston, via one of the Jewish hotels in Millis. Rabbi Pinchus David Horowitz, also born in Poland, known to Jews as the Bostoner Rebbe, had come to Millis for a week's vacation one summer after World War I. He was impressed with Joseph Mael's piety, and in turn my zayde became his disciple, making periodic trips to his home on Columbia Road, Dorchester. For his entire life he learned with Pinchus David Horowitz and his son, Levi Yitzhak Horowitz, who succeeded his father as the Bostoner Rebbe, who would become well known even outside of Jewish Boston. The first American-born Hasidic Rebbe, Levi Yitzhak Horowitz became renowned by opening his large home to generations of Orthodox Jewish students at Harvard and MIT and to many a religious family far from home whose loved one was being treated in one of Boston's world-famous hospitals. Even as he acquired his fame, this Bostoner Rebbe, who would live until 2009, always had time for his very observant country-peddler-become-farmer-acolyte Joseph Mael, and the extended Mael family in Millis.

The Maels multiplied in the 1920s and 1930s with four sons, Harry, Morris, Edward, and Mark, and a daughter, Helen, all but one of whom lived in Millis, in houses across or down Village Street from the Mael shul. His two oldest sons became cattle dealers, buying and selling cows (and milk) much as Zayde traded in chickens. The Mael children had large families of their own, with wonderfully colorful nicknames: Leon was Label, Seymour was Shleme, Nysen was Nysie, Sydney was Simkie, Joshua was Puffy, Mildred was Malkie, Ruth was Aukie, Kenneth was Kissie, Melvin was Mottie, Francis was Sickie, and Evelyn was Evie. So by the time I arrived in Millis there was always a minyan of ten men on Shabbos (Sabbath) and Jewish holidays made up primarily of three generations of Mael men, a few others from Millis and Medway like Maurie Merkin and Coleman Finkelstein, and the occasional summer visitor from one of the hotels. Bubby Etta's family, which had originally brought the couple to "the country," had moved to Boston in the interwar years, and there was little contact between the two families thereafter. Joseph's children and grandchildren were as deeply religious (and Republican) as he was. No Mael drove, worked, carried anything, or put on lights during the Shabbos. There was a *Shabbos goy*, a Christian neighbor named Leo Braun, who would come by to turn on or off the electricity or the stove. Four sets of dishes were used, regular dairy and meat and Passover *milchadich* and *fleishich*.

Only Zayde Mael's daughter, Helen, had no children. Born in Medway three years after her parents came to America, my foster mother was to be the first of Zayde's children to finish twelve grades of school, as her two older brothers, Harry and Morris, had left school in the ninth and seventh grade. After graduation she went to the Jewish Seminary in Cincinnati, but its unexpected reform (non-Orthodox) orientation and the need for her at home brought her quickly back to Millis. As the only daughter she was expected to do chores that her often infirm mother, Etta, could not do. She was married in 1936 at the age of twenty-nine to Saul Spiro, then thirty-six.

It seemed a perfect match. She was a bright, attractive, and imposing dark-haired woman from a proudly religious family. He was a good-looking, tall, and well-built man who had been born in Poland, apparently to a family of some means, and who often talked of having had a governess in his early years. Like so many of his generation, he came to America alone, leaving behind parents who, alas, would perish in the Holocaust. He settled in Boston, because his uncle was superintendent of that city's Jewish Home for the Aged. With little formal education, Saul took a job in the millinery trade in Boston. Apparently, Helen had made a good catch: the nephew of a prominent professional in the Boston Jewish community and, she thought, a devoutly observant Jew.

In Millis, Saul was absorbed into the large Mael extended family. Taken into his father-in-law's chicken business, he and Helen rented the first floor of a two-story house. My foster mother's younger brother Eddy, his wife Esther, and their four daughters, Marilyn, Barbie, Roberta, and Nancy, rented the apartment upstairs. This house was separated by a small pasture from the larger house owned by Helen's two older brothers, Morris and Harry, who also lived upstairs and downstairs with their large families. The families shared two houses and one party-line telephone number. Each had a phone fixed to the wall with no dial. To make a call one cranked a lever on the side of the phone box, and when the operator responded with "Number please?" you said "One six one ring three" if you wanted Eddie's phone. To receive calls, one had to count the number of rings. The Spiros' number was "One six one ring one."

My lucky break was that Helen and Saul had no children, and that in the fall of 1943, when she was thirty-six and Saul forty-three, Zayde heard from someone that the state was looking for a Jewish foster home for a five-year-old boy. So I was transported to this strange and supportive place—part Norman Rockwell, with fields, pastures, chickens, and cows, and part old-world Sholom Aleichem, with Yiddish-speaking men wearing *yarmulkas* and *talleisim* (prayer shawls), swaying as they *davened* (prayed) every Shabbos in the simple village shul.

It wasn't by any means clear, of course, when I arrived in November 1943 that I would stay long in Millis. I did because Helen Spiro, my tenacious foster mother, won what would be a multiyear tug-of-war over me with the usually less combative Max, and with the Commonwealth of Massachusetts, which was at times angry with Helen but amazed at how unlike their other foster mothers she turned out to be. My new foster mother would be the clear winner and very much on her own terms. A formidable and resolute presence, she dominates every page in the file for my years in Millis. She fought with the state over every dime and dollar she thought was owed to me; she laid down the law to Max; she manhandled Millis town officials; she argued with heads of hospitals. There would certainly be self-serving aspects in these epic encounters, but she emerged my loyal advocate, who provided a secure, if not warm, home for me.

The struggle began the day I arrived in Millis. My first memory, for this is where I, through memory, begin to inhabit this narrative, is of the Mael clan gathering to meet me and welcome back Shleme, who was home from the war on a brief furlough. I remember his uniform, but not the war. In retrospect I realize with amazement how little we talked in rural Millis about the war or its significance for Jews in those years. In December 1942, the British government had announced publicly for the first time the staggering dimensions of Hitler's policy of exterminating European Jewry, but there was little open talk of it in Washington and certainly not in quiet, bucolic Millis. All this notwithstanding, etched in my memory is my new GI "cousin," sharing the spotlight with me. What I don't remember is that I was also sick that night, so sick and so scared that I apparently fell asleep only after I clambered into bed with Saul. Helen skewered the social workers for bringing her a sick child who required a doctor's care. Meanwhile, the state was not above using my delicate health to persuade the potentially problematic Max to postpone his first visit.

As you know this child has been removed from Mrs. Bell's home. It was not easy to secure a good boarding home for Isaac. He was removed so recently that it is not wise to send you a permit to visit until the period of adjustment for both the child and the new foster mother has had more opportunity to develop. He is in a good foster home in Millis. This couple have never had State Wards in their home before. I do not wish to lose this home at this time, so it would be wiser to wait another month or six weeks before visiting. As you know he had a severe cold in Mrs. Bell's home and the new foster mother is taking on quite a job in caring for this little boy, I don't want her to get discouraged and give this boy up at this time, as he is in need of a good home.

Coping with sickly Isaac was a persistent theme of my first years in Millis, causing continuous friction between the state and my foster mother and providing the source, I am sure, of much of the early bonding between Helen and me. Concerned with my recurring fevers and difficulty in putting on weight, Mrs. Bell had hoped that removal of my tonsils would end my troubles. They were taken out just before I left her care in a three-day hospital stay. But my health problems had only just begun. In my first two weeks in Millis, Helen had Drs. Zalvin and Sheinkopf examine me at the house three times.

Fig. 5 | Young Isaac in Millis, MA

Convinced that my respiratory infections were more serious than these local doctors realized, Helen persuaded the reluctant social worker to approve a trip to a heart specialist in Framingham, some fifteen miles away. For the next three years, managing my "heart condition" absorbed much of her time and energy. I in turn emerged from the ordeal for all intents and purposes her son.

The specialist reported evidence of low-grade rheumatic fever and recommended I be hospitalized for further study and treatment. Helen then pestered the state to arrange an evaluation at Boston's prestigious Massachusetts General Hospital four months after I had been brought to Millis. The experts at Mass General discovered a slight murmur but told Helen I would outgrow it and suggested she deal with me as a normal child. Helen still was not satisfied. She convinced the state visitor to authorize a follow-up every three months at this Mass General clinic. These checkups were all-day affairs, commencing with a long bus ride from Millis to the start of Boston's subway line at Forest Hills, then an MTA trolley ride to Charles Street, and finally a walk to the hospital. Once we made it through the seemingly endless corridors, waiting rooms, and dead ends we arrived at the clinic, sitting for what seemed like forever with other mothers and children on hard wooden chairs in rows until my name was called. We always brought sandwiches from Millis because Helen ate only kosher food. But my foster mother was a force to contend with on these excursions, pushing herself forward on the subway and with head nurses.

I found the clinic trips magical. As the noisy subway sped through the dark tunnels, I saw myself reflected in windows transformed into mirrors. I was thrilled when the nurses called out *Isaac Kramnick*, even though they usually mispronounced my name. These trips to Boston and Helen's worrying about my health allowed her to feel that she was much the better parent to me than the state. The trips tied me to her as well. I held her hand as we made our way through the city. When she told strangers that she was my mother, I felt safer and more secure than ever before.

Visits to Mass General in 1944 confirmed that I was a normal kid, so I began the first grade that September at age six, in the part of the twelve-grade school building set aside for the elementary school. But that spring, just after my seventh birthday, I developed scarlet fever and was taken to the Massachusetts Memorial Hospital for a three-week stay, fearful that I might not be returned to Millis. Shortly after my return to Millis, on a routine check-up at the Mass General cardiac clinic I was seen, through the luck of the doctor's rotation, by Paul Dudley White, Boston's eminent heart specialist and one of the founders of the American Heart Association. He was just another man in a long white coat to me, but Helen regaled everyone on Village Street again and again with word that this great man had looked at my heart.

I was too young to perceive it, but Helen must have felt some small sense of vindication when Dr. White pronounced it probable that I had developed rheumatic fever after the attack of scarlet fever and recommended that I be confined to bed, preferably at a sanatorium. When Dr. Paul Dudley White spoke, the Commonwealth of Massachusetts moved. So it was that short of two years after I was placed in Millis, had started school, and had begun to think of the Spiros and the Maels as my family, I was taken away once again, this time to the Sharon Sanatorium, where I remained for five months.

Fig. 6 |
Isaac at the Sharon
Sanatorium, 1943

Ten miles from Millis, now a fashionable suburb of Boston, Sharon in 1945 was another town of farms and fields. The sanatorium, founded in 1890 for children with tuberculosis, was a compound of several long low stucco buildings surrounded by deep woods. My building had wooden steps leading up to a large front door and a porch the width of the building, where, after my first six weeks of being confined to bed, I often happily sat on a rocking chair. Presiding over this peaceful place was Miss Terry, an affable middle-aged woman whom the patients, all children, liked and feared. My only run-in with Miss Terry was over rhubarb. Perhaps because it flourished in the sanatorium's garden or was deemed magic food for strong hearts, rhubarb was a staple at Sharon. Although I hated it—and still do—Miss Terry made me eat it, mixing it with ice cream to make it more palatable.

The sanatorium had a small school in one of its buildings, where, after I was ambulatory, I did my second-grade schoolwork alongside children completing assignments appropriate for their age. I looked forward to this part of the day and the teacher's constant attention.

First grade in Millis had been a disaster. Miss Hartigan smacked our knuckles with a ruler, which she stopped doing only when my foster mother complained to the principal after having caught her in the act one day when she was taking me out of school for a doctor's appointment. At the sanatorium I flourished in ways second graders do, and I have often wondered whether this cozy introduction shaped my enjoyment of school in the years to come.

But a cloud hung over these months in Sharon, and it was a dark one. What would happen to me when I left? Helen, and sometimes Saul, visited on many Sundays, but I worried that I might not go back to Millis. I detected serious friction between Helen and the sanatorium administration, who often found her difficult. My social worker reported for the file Miss Terry's request that my foster mother send some clothing for me to the sanatorium:

> States they took up the matter of clothing with foster mother and she was not at all cooperative, stating she did not intend to spend money for clothing when the boy was not in her home. They have not been at all pleased with her attitude. She is quite demanding, wants privileges of visiting at times different from other people, criticizes everything that is done. They feel that child's attitude expresses fear of her. She talks at great length to them about her fondness for the boy but is always telling them how much she gives up in order to visit him on Sundays.

Given the wartime shortage of help, the sanatorium asked parents to take laundry home one week and return it the next. The visitor notes, "She has refused to take his laundry and do it at home as other mothers do. Explains her lack of interest in taking his washing home as natural because she does no laundry anyway, sending it out." My caseworker must have intervened, for as my convalescence ended, Helen had grown more cooperative, taking my laundry and even bringing me a snowsuit. Still, it was not until the day I left Sharon, in the car with Helen and Saul, that I knew I was returning to Millis.

Just before I was released, Miss Terry wrote to my caseworker that "when Isaac returns to his foster home he will not be under a restrictive routine but will be able to live a completely normal life."

But neither Miss Terry nor the social worker had counted on Helen, who insisted, on the contrary, that I needed special treatment. She took on the whole town of Millis to get her way, precipitating a "school bus war" when I returned home.

Insisting that my heart was too weak for me to walk the fifth of a mile to the school bus stop serving our neighborhood, Helen refused to send me to school until the bus picked me up directly in front of our house. Pearly Eaton, the supercilious superintendent of schools, who insisted that everyone call him Dr. Eaton, feared a precedent that would open the door to parents who wanted to reduce the 1,100-foot maximum distance from a school bus stop. The bus, he decreed, would not pick me up at home. Meanwhile, Mr. Brown, the peacemaking principal, tried to finesse the issue by picking me up in his own car on his way to work. I came to admire Clyde Brown, not only for this generous gesture but for his honesty and decency when I dealt with him as a student leader in high school. He was the kind of craggy, laconic, commonsensical Yankee whom the media today love to interview just before the New Hampshire presidential primary. But Dr. Eaton was not impressed; he ordered Mr. Brown to cease and desist. Helen dug in her heels, too. As stalemate loomed, she upped the ante. Not only would she keep me out of school, she informed the superintendent, but she intended to present her complaint at the annual town meeting scheduled for the following week.

I was mortified by the whole affair. Having only recently come to town, I knew few kids well. And since I had done well in the sanatorium school, when I came back from Sharon at mid–school year, I had been put into Millis's third grade, where I knew no one. I squirmed in school when I was called the "state kid" and felt embarrassed that my last name was different from my public champions, the Spiros. Now I had become different in yet another way. My "cousins" upstairs could walk to the bus stop, but I assumed everyone in school was thinking I was too weak and sickly. Arriving at school in the principal's car surely didn't endear me to my classmates.

Concerned that the Jews of Millis, fifty families strong, might all show up at the town meeting to support one of their own, Superintendent Eaton contacted the Sharon Sanatorium, whereupon the redoubtable Miss Terry told him that I was perfectly able to walk that distance twice a day, especially since it was a level road with a hard surface. "He would not have been discharged from the San. had he not been able to attend public school and to get there on his own two feet." Indeed, it would be good for me to do what other children did "rather than be singled out as an invalid." Presented with his findings and the threat to make them public at the town meeting, Helen backed down. I walked to the bus stop, and the annual Millis town meeting was spared a debate over my health. I still cringe, however, when I think of the concession made by the school in return: I was granted special time each day for a year to rest in the nurse's room!

During the "school bus war," my caseworkers sided with the school authorities despite repeated descriptions of me during these months as "thin," "delicate," "fragile," and "looking rather pathetic." "Wr. fos. mo. advising that I. was sent home and into community to take up normal life again and with understanding that he could do as other chn. do. Therefore we feel that no exception can be made by Dept. to make spec. transportation arrangements for I. to attend school."

My foster mother moved on to new health fronts, insisting that I needed special orthopedic shoes, glasses, allergy shots, and extra dental work. Each request led to lengthy wrangling with the state and further embarrassment for me, since Helen often took me out of school for these medical forays. To her credit, though, her insistent nurturing care turned a fragile five-year-old into a healthy boy. And it made her a mother. Rescuing sickly Isaac enhanced her sense of me as her son and my sense of her as my mother. Upstairs and down the street her brothers and sisters-in-law had families; so too, now, did she. Inevitably, of course, these developments created problems with Max, and, it turned out, with the state, for whom this was becoming a very unusual foster home.

The state was incredulous, for example, when Helen summarily announced that she intended to enroll me in school as "Isaac Spiro," since, as she put it, "that's how I was known around town." Despite the caseworker's notation that she was "very persistent in getting her way on this matter," she didn't. The Division's head office in Boston ruled that she had to use my real name. Defeated but unfazed, my foster mother put her imprint on me by calling me Sonny. The name stuck. I was Sonny Kramnick to everyone who knew me long after I left Millis. To my foster parents and the Maels I was in those years "Sonny Spiro."

Helen moved resourcefully on another front, as well, in her campaign to eliminate signs that I was not hers. She asked the state to have Max's visits with me take place at the Division of Child Guardianship's Boston State House office rather than in Millis, where presumably his coming and going would be visible to everyone on Village Street. Again the state said no, pointing out that Max had the right to see his child in the home in which he had been placed. Helen managed to win a partial victory, once again, laying down strict rules, which my social worker did not challenge, about the frequency and advance notice of Max's visits.

Despite this concession, the state made it clear in these early Millis years that I was a child of the state. When my foster mother surprisingly expressed a wish to adopt me shortly after I arrived, the state advised against it, citing my father's continued interest in me and the fact that the "boy's mother is insane and the boy himself is a rheumatic heart case." While I was in the sanatorium, and Miss Terry reported problems with Helen, the state suggested to Helen that she might not want to take me back when I recovered. My social worker, it seems, believed that Helen was ambivalent about me. While she said she loved me and claimed that no foster mother did half as much as she did for her state child, my foster mother added that my presence had dramatically changed her life, but not always for the better. After all, she now had to get up early to give me breakfast and trips to Sharon often upset her weekend plans. To this outburst the social worker responded that "it might be that this boy was too much care for you and that while he was in the hospital it might be a good time to think the matter over carefully, and if it would be better for Isaac, plan to have him placed elsewhere when he was ready for discharge." Helen shot back that the social worker should learn more about "Isaac's feeling for her" before making a decision.

Little did I know what was at stake the day the social worker visited me at the sanatorium and casually asked what I thought about

Millis and the Spiros. Petrified that I was yet again to be abandoned and moved to another family, I described my "sincere attachment for foster parents and a strong desire to remain in their house." I realize now that Helen needed that signal, too, that affirmation of my feelings for her. No surprise, then, that Helen's aggressive manner with Miss Terry abruptly changed, the state stopped considering a new placement, and the social worker noted "foster mother is sincerely fond of boy and is willing to do everything she can for him."

"Everything" included further shootouts and turf wars with the state. My foster mother and the state were locked in what one caseworker called "constant commercial haggling." She wanted more and better clothes for me than the foster care provision allowed. She demanded money for medical and dental care far above the state's frugal allotments. If the division ruled that that my cavities had to be filled by school dentists, Helen lobbied for treatment by her family dentist, Dr. Pinsky. She fought for snowsuits, second pairs of glasses, and special shoes. When the state's auditors questioned reimbursement requests for trips to Boston, Helen erupted that the authorities had no right to deny her boy a nice pair of slacks to wear to shul.

The state was particularly upset at my foster mother's indifference to regulations requiring that estimates be sent to Boston so that medical treatments or extraordinary clothing purchases could be authorized ahead of time. A social worker wrote, bluntly, in 1948 that "foster mother apparently has used her own judgment over the years regarding Isaac. She seems to have no responsibility towards the Division regarding any policy concerning the Division and the boy." The visitor added, gratuitously, that Helen used the name Spiro for me and "that her friends and acquaintances do not know that the boy is not her own."

Helen expected that the state would pay for summer camp, for Hebrew school tuition, for swimming lessons. Her middle-class sense of what kind of clothes, health care, and privileges her son should have clashed repeatedly with the state's conventional class assumptions about foster care, with its down-market budgets. But while the state frequently could not believe Helen's chutzpah and was particularly annoyed with her constant haggling over money, it always held back, acknowledging, if grudgingly, that she was an exceptionally good foster mother. The file is full of notations that "this is a very good home," that "Isaac has many advantages in this home," that "living conditions are very good." When I was nine and Helen complained that neither the state nor Max appreciated the care she was providing me, the social worker wrote, "It seems apparent that Mrs. S. has problems of her own, but she does give I. good care and, in her own way, she is fond of him. It seems desirable for the Division to give Mrs. S. a certain amount of recognition, praise for her efforts with I. and acknowledge definite appreciations of the care she's given him."

I knew nothing at the time about these struggles over money or clothes; only years later did I learn that my foster parents received money for raising me. I did, however, have some sense of the good care I was receiving. And when I forgot, Helen was quick to remind me that Mrs. Bell fed me nothing but hot dogs and beans. I grew comfortable in the Spiro house. I knew full well that I was not technically their son; the difference in names made that obvious. But I answered readily to Sonny Kramnick at school and to Sonny Spiro at home, on Village Street, and around the Maels. As I played with friends and "cousins" or spent my time at school I pushed these familial issues out of mind. Except, of course, when Max came to Millis.

The Spiros never referred to Max as "your father." He was always "Mr. Kramnick" or "old man Kramnick." In his mid-sixties in these years, Max visited about every six months. The occasions were fraught with tension and fear. In the days before he arrived, Helen belittled him: he was unreliable; he had the effrontery to make the journey on Saturday, when good Jews didn't travel. I didn't need her to tear him down; I dreaded the visits, since they made manifest the anomalies of my life, which I preferred to submerge.

My father usually arrived early in the afternoon, after a long journey by bus or train from Peabody to Boston, a subway across the city, and a bus ride to Millis. Helen and Saul hovered around the house as the time drew near for his arrival. I was noticeably nervous. When he entered the house, there were a few awkward moments that seemed to last forever as the four of us sat together, and then the Spiros left us alone for a while. No food or tea was served. My memories of Max come from these visits, since I recall nothing of him in the first five years of my life. He was a short man with a tiny face, eyes that could twinkle, a small chin, and tight facial muscles around a small mouth. I recall vividly his day-old stubble, since he always kissed me when he left, a gesture I found particularly unsettling. The Spiros were not physically demonstrative people, and I was not used to being kissed or hugged.

His voice was soft and gentle, though this did not endear him to me. Our stilted conversations were usually about school or sports. He never spoke with me about my brothers or my mother, nor, for that matter, did the Spiros or the social workers. And I certainly never asked about a mother; two fathers and Helen seemed more than enough. Nor, for that matter, did I know I had living "real" brothers. It would be years, then, before I could appreciate how difficult these visits to me must have been for Max, sandwiched as they were between more frequent visits to his wife and oldest son, both then inmates at the more nearby Danvers State Hospital. I cannot imagine now how painful it must have been for Max to see Sarah and Leon in the neo-Gothic pile of Hathorne Hill that locals still called the "State Lunatic Hospital." And he did it for years.

Mother and son probably never saw each other in their confinement. The state hospital at Danvers was a massive structure built in 1878, with eight long wings radiating off a central administrative unit in what was then a park-like rural setting of hundreds of acres. The inspiration for the hospital's rural setting was Dr. Thomas Story Kirkbride, its first superintendent and the man after whom its huge central building was named. He had made a legendary reputation as head of the Pennsylvania hospital for decades, believing that beautiful settings, fresh air, and sunshine brought patients out of their delusions and restored a more natural "balance of the senses."

Men and women were at different ends of the complex, and Max had to go the lengthy distance from one to the other on visiting days. A sense of how huge the place was is apparent in realizing that when it was closed in 1992 and the buildings razed in 2006, 497 condo apartments were built on only a small part of its former footprint.

Even the meager psychiatric speculation that could be made of her early days of confinement disappears from my mother's hospital file in these years. The notations are infrequent and spare: "eating poorly . . . very unattentive . . . very rambling . . . unusually destructive . . . assumes flirtatious manners . . . silly expressions . . . appears euphoric . . . depressed and unhappy." She seems never to have been seen by any professional psychiatric staff, to have received any therapeutic treatment, or to have been observed by doctors. Her record has no entries assessing her status, let alone discussions of improvement, decline, or chances for discharge. She was simply Patient No. 36669, "a short moderately obese middle-aged woman often speaking to herself in Yiddish," housed with over 2,300 others and cared for in 1945 by a night shift of nine people in a horribly overcrowded institution originally intended for a maximum of 600 patients.

While her file provides little sense of my mother's time at Danvers after the late 1930s, I have nothing whatsoever on Leon's life after he came there in 1942. I have not been able to retrieve his Danvers file and do not know whether he received any of the three principal treatments given to hospitalized schizophrenics in the 1940s. Most common was the injection of large amounts of insulin to induce shock and occasionally comas. Pioneered by the Viennese psychiatrist Manfred Sakel in the late 1920s, "shock therapy" became widespread in American mental hospitals in the 1940s. The fits and spasms that followed the shock and comas were ended by intravenously administered glucose. Not as common, since it required great surgical skill, but perceived to provide more spectacular results, were frontal lobotomies, which in the 1940s were performed at some fifteen sites in the United States.

The preferred treatment in Massachusetts when my mother and brother were hospitalized was electroconvulsive therapy. Electric shock therapy, as it was more commonly called, was invented in 1938 by Ugo Cerletti, head of the psychiatry department at the University of Rome, who developed the procedure on animals first. Introduced to American hospitals in 1940, it quickly spread as the radical new treatment for schizophrenia. Patients, often restrained or tied down, whose informed consent was irrelevant, were often given electric shocks on multiple occasions. They responded with seizures and convulsions, and then loss of consciousness, as the brainwaves in the cerebral cortex fell silent. It often took weeks after the patient came to for brain-wave activity to return to normal, but what happened in most cases was substantial diminution of intellectual and cognitive capacity and a dulling of emotional intensity. The "curative" benefit was a parallel decline in patient fantasies, delusions, and paranoia. Wards also became easier to manage, even as most inmates soon returned to their earlier psychotic symptoms. More than likely Leon received Dr. Cerletti's therapy, since the last words of the papers committing him to Danvers recommend "maybe considered for electro-shock therapy."

Max had some companionship in these years; Sigmund lived with him in the apartment on 3 Little's Lane in their four rooms: a kitchen, a living room, and two bedrooms. While Max worked long hours at Samuel Tarlow's leather factory for $50 a week, Sigmund enjoyed high school. He played trumpet in the band and was a very good student. In his senior year, and by then called Ziggy, he was one of eight at Peabody High School to win a National Merit Scholarship. He entered Boston University as a commuter in 1948 but lasted only six months. He was in love. He had met Helen Machires, a Greek girl, in high school while both had jobs after school in a Salem Foodland. Helen worked in the deli and Ziggy in the grocery. Helen's dad, Socrates, called Socko by everyone, worked in a Peabody leather factory. After dropping out of Boston University, Ziggy and Helen eloped to New Hampshire and lived apart until Helen mastered the courage to tell her father that she was married. Socko told her that because she had married a non-Greek, she was no longer his daughter. Max had no problem with either a nonwedding or a non-Jewish wife but was bothered by having to live alone, since the newlyweds rented a one-room apartment in Salem. Socko came around eventually to the apartment and to the marriage when Ziggy converted to Greek Orthodoxy.

Of course, I had no idea of the existence of Leon or Ziggy in my early years in Millis, nor, as I have said, of my mother either, only of Max. No siblings then, but thinking about this today, I wonder why I was not curious about my biological mother as I was growing up, unlike orphaned or separated boys and girls in storybooks

Fig. 7 |
Helen and Saul
Spiro, Isaac's foster
parents

who seem to constantly brood over a lost parent. It was massive
avoidance and denial, I'm sure, but also enabling and empowering.
I was neither introspective nor given to daydreaming as I grew up in
Millis. I didn't dwell on my Dickensian odyssey before I was plunked
down with the Spiros. I played, and I was happy. I did not consciously
lament something lost or missing. I had never seen a picture of this
woman, my "real" mother. No one told me stories about her that I
could cherish in quiet reveries. I don't think I avoided thinking of
her from anger. She simply didn't exist, didn't matter.

On his visits Max never asked if I were happy in Millis, nor did
I volunteer anything so personal. And he certainly didn't ask me if
I wanted to live with him. After an hour or so of strained and desul-
tory conversation, Helen always reappeared to announce that "Mr.
Kramnick" should head back to the bus stop. Although I cringed,
he would kiss me on his way out and put some candy or a dollar
bill in my hand, sometimes both. After he left, Helen pumped me
about what we talked about, and I seldom obliged, preferring to

run outside the house and forget the whole experience. I forgot him quickly and didn't think of him until the next visit was announced.

Helen, however, worried constantly about Max and his legal right to reclaim me. Ironically, she would herself unwittingly precipitate a crisis that almost led the state to return me to him, even as my foster care seemed seamlessly to merge with normal family life. I was eleven and twelve when this tug-of-war cleared the air, dramatically and stressfully, of the uncertainty that hovered over my first years in Millis.

My foster parents were under considerable pressure in 1949 and 1950. Helen and Saul had been evicted from the downstairs apartment on Village Street. Wartime rent controls had been abandoned and George Viener, the landlord, had raised the rent. The Spiros refused to pay and were kicked out. In haste, they found an apartment on Main Street near the town center. I remember it as a strange place with a sunken kitchen and rooms that curled unexpectedly around the top floor of a large barn-like building that had a small store on its first floor. This dwelling was light years from Helen's conception of a proper house. Worse yet, it was far from the Mael family houses and shul on Village Street. Adding to these concerns was the uncertainty of Helen's plans for my bar mitzvah, which loomed as the moment when, along with me, she would be showcased before family and community as Sonny's mother. Hebrew lessons were now two miles away. And where would people go for the kiddush after my performance in shul?

Helen was also under pressure from the state. Having only learned of my new address from Mr. Brown at school, the Division of Child Guardianship was furious that she didn't notify them that we had moved. At the next visit, my social worker told my foster mother that "while she might regard me as her own son, the state was still legally my real parent." Offering no regrets, Helen repeated her resentments at the state for not giving her the right to use her own judgment about my welfare. Then she turned to what really troubled her: a nagging, fearful suspicion that Max would take me away after all the years she had given me, after all the sacrifices she had made for me as her son, and, not surprisingly, all the expense for my religious education.

In the spring of 1950, Helen's temper, unleashed perhaps by the strain she was under, annoyed Max so much that he made the dreaded move: he insisted on his right to have me back. He had written on two consecutive weekends announcing a visit to the new house on Main Street and both times had failed to show up. The first time he claimed he had a backache; the second time it was raining. On neither occasion had he called Millis about his change of plans. Helen was livid because we had stayed in both days waiting for him, and when he arrived on a subsequent Saturday, she told him off. Max said he could not understand why waiting a few hours was such a problem. After all, he only visited twice a year. I then weighed in. Already in the anxious, tense mood that always accompanied these visits, I couldn't stand listening to Helen's attack on Max or his feeble, shouted-down rebuttals. I asked my foster mother for permission to leave and watch the Red Sox game on a friend's TV. She agreed. Max was enraged, not without reason, when I fled the scene. No surprise, then, that after he returned to Peabody he wrote to Boston seeking my immediate return to him.

The state's response was a full-scale inquiry into my future, involving an interview with me and Helen in the Division of Child Guardianship's office in Boston's State House, as well as a visit by a social worker to Max in Peabody. In Boston, Helen

> expressed some concern about whether the father might provide a home for Isaac and take him out of her home after all the years she has given him. Fo. mo. states that the boy feels as though he were their own son. Went on to say that the boy and the father were almost strangers. Father has only visited once or twice a year and the time he spends with the boy consists of only a few minutes. It was obvious that the boy did not know just what to say to his father and that he was getting bored. Boy did not look forward to his fathers visit but on the contrary she feels he may dread them.

He calls her "mother." She would feel awful "if I were sent back to old man Kramnick," who would never give me the care she did. The

uncertainty about me, she told the social worker, left her not knowing what to do with the bar mitzvah plans, or what size apartment
or house she and Saul should look for as they left the downtown
Main Street apartment.

It was then my turn.

Visitor arranged to talk with Isaac in private. Explained to Isaac
the father's plans for taking him home. Visitor wanted to know
about Isaac's feelings relative to this. The boy was able to say that
he wanted very much to stay in foster home, that he was sure he
would not be happy with father. Does not know the town where
father lives or any of the people. Isaac wanted to stay with foster
parents just as long as he possibly could. Visitor told Isaac that
the father would be visiting and the boy could speak to him about
his feelings but that this department would have to go along with
father's plan.

In the preceding few days, Helen, who was a wonderful cook,
had not so subtly campaigned by predicting that in Peabody my
menu would be limited, as with Mrs. Bell's, to hot dogs and baked
beans. She need not have worried; she already had my vote—and
my allegiance. I certainly preferred Spiros and Maels to the man
with the stubbly face, the virtual stranger who visited twice a year.
I was adamant: "He, himself says three times during the conversation that he does not want to live with his father." I wanted to live
with "my mother and dad, and with my friends."

The social worker then visited Peabody, where he was unexpectedly impressed with the size and appearance of the apartment on
3 Little's Lane. Sigmund, who had finished school but not yet married, was out working in a bottling company, and only Max was
interviewed. He volunteered that he was "tired of being pushed
out of Isaac's life" by Mrs. Spiro. In response to an oddly paired set
of questions, he allowed that he neither drank nor attended Jewish
services regularly, though he promised to do the latter if I were
returned. The social worker pressed him on the undesirability of
a twelve-year-old boy being home alone during school vacations
while Max worked in the leather mill from seven in the morning

to four in the afternoon. Sigmund "had done just fine" in that situation, Max replied, and had graduated Peabody High School with honors.

Meanwhile, I seem to have taken matters into my own hands. When Max next visited and we were alone, instead of fidgeting impatiently through his questions about school, I told him plainly that I didn't want to leave my foster parents to live with him. He sat quietly, as he often did, and then after a few minutes said simply, "All right. If that's what you want." He never pressed the issue again.

Finally free of the cycle of abandonment and rescue, I was jubilant at the resolution of the yearlong crisis. I was now definitively Helen and Saul's son. I pushed out of mind thoughts about biological parents and social workers. I didn't think of myself as a foster child, but, like my many cousins in Millis, as part of the extended Mael family. Max's gracious retreat helped, of course. His interests in me were mercurial at best, and during this crisis they were stoked more by fury with Helen than by ardor for me. But in the end he did consider my interests.

Even more important, I had for the first time taken some control of my fate—and helped engineer a solution. I didn't realize it at the time, but it may well have been a pivotal moment in my emotional development.

My file reveals that this crisis had been further complicated for everyone, except unknowing me, by the possibility of adoption. Convinced by its inquiry that the best outcome for me was Millis, the state had seized upon a passing remark that Helen had made in the Boston interview. She said that when I first came to Millis she had wanted to adopt me and had been talked out of pursuing it by the state. Did she want to go that route now, the state asked, since a new law had just lowered the age of choice from fourteen to twelve in contested adoptions? Wary of such a dramatic step, Helen answered that she needed to talk it over with her husband. Some weeks later Helen told the social worker of their decision.

Visitor was able to talk with fo. mo. separately relative to possible adoption of the boy inasmuch as the new law makes this possible in spite of parents' objection. She stated that she and her husband have discussed this at some length and decided not to go ahead.

Foster mother stated they felt the insanity in boy's family was hereditary. Isaac's mother is in a mental hospital, she said and she has a brother or sister who is also mentally ill. In addition to this fact, she explained, there is another Kramnick child older than Isaac who formerly lived in Millis in foster home who is in an institution.

Taking a very different stance than it had when I was five, the state, while not correcting Helen's inaccurate account of my family, did an about-face and tried to convince Helen to pursue the adoption.

Visitor stated that there was reason to doubt whether there was any hereditary strain in the family. That most of our knowledge today fairly discounts the idea that mental illnesses are transmitted from parents to the child. Foster mother, however, did not seem to accept this.

But she did agree to postpone a final decision for a few months. Meanwhile, my case was assigned to a new social worker, who wrote three months later:

Mrs. Spiro was quite anxious to unburden her concerns upon the new visitor. She stated the usual complaints of unnecessary delay in paying bills, low clothing allowance, etc. After this introduction, Visitor discussed the matter of adoption with her. Foster mother stated that they are no longer interested in adoption since Sonny regarded them as his parents anyway, and she feels that in a few years he will be grown and possibly leaving their household and she felt that the purpose of having a child had been fulfilled by his stay until this time. It was quite evident that the real reason she is not interested in adoption is the matter of insanity in the family background.

When I read as an adult about my foster mother's decision not to adopt me I was angry. It would have cleared the air, regularizing my life then and forever after. But the academic in me wonders whether it wasn't, in fact, exactly what a rational person should have chosen: stick to the status quo. Max was no longer a threat. Our relationship was already openly and evidently as parents and son. I would, in all likelihood, be leaving their home in a few years. Why adopt when there was a remote chance of hereditary mental problems? Why adopt when doing so would end the cash assistance provided by state board payments? Her choice was not an unreasonable one, assuming, of course, as she probably did, that my feelings about being adopted were not an issue. And assuming, as she undoubtedly did, that I did not—and would not—know that she had declined to end my life as a foster child.

CHAPTER 4

Helen and Saul

What I didn't know, then, didn't hurt me; all that mattered was the stability and security I found with the Spiros. That life with them lacked warmth and affection, that theirs was a troubled marriage in a sterile home, was deeply disturbing to me as I grew up, but it seemed a small price to pay for being settled. The source of their troubles was that Saul never lived up to the promise of the match, and a deeply disappointed and unhappy Helen found herself living with a crude and unpredictable embarrassment.

Saul was a vulgar, loutish man, capable of swearing viciously in Yiddish, Polish, and English. Uneducated and unlearned, he had no hobbies or interests. I never saw him read a book, though he did read newspapers and watch TV, complaining all the time that the shows were "repeats." A sullen man, he found conversations difficult and seemed to enjoy only playing cards, mostly solitaire or occasionally pinochle. He smoked cheap nickel cigars, whose paper rings I loved to play with, and he drank too much—not at home, but usually on public occasions, intensifying all the more the shame for Helen and me.

Especially excruciating was his occasional drunkenness at the lovely kiddush that sometimes followed shul to mark a special *simchah*, a happy occasion like a holiday, birthday, or baby naming. In a little parade, Zayde, my uncles, cousins, Saul, and I crossed Village Street to Harry's downstairs dining room, where Aunt Nelly, whom I adored, had spread on the table her delicious mandel bread, ruggelah, and sweet kugels. After the *brachah*, the blessing, over the wine, the men drank a small shot of *schnapps*, usually Canadian Club rye whiskey, to salute the occasion. Standing beside him I saw that while everyone was busily eating the *lockshen kugel*, the noodle pudding, Saul reached again for the bottle. "No dad; that's enough," I whispered. But one of my mischievous older cousins, eager to provoke a scene, caught the move, too. "Here Saul, you deserve another," he'd offer, handing him the liquor. Fearing what was about to happen, I'd tug his jacket and plead, "No more; let's go home." "Zayde is two-faced," he'd blurt out, ignoring me while speaking to the nearest relative. Sensing the potential for post-services fun and games, another cousin offered a third drink, while asking, almost as an aside, "So how is Zayde two-faced, Saul?" "Because," Saul replied, raising the volume a bit, "he complains that the hotel Jews are not really *frum*[religious] enough, yet he takes their goyische money for the shul on Rosh Hashonah." By this time everyone around the table was listening, the cousins who had egged him on had quietly moved away, and Zayde stormed out of the room, leaving me at Saul's side, at once sheepish and furious with him and my troublemaking cousins. Having let off steam, Saul then became a jolly drunk, calmly walking a mortified me home while always offering the same folk wisdom: "A drink makes you feel like a new man, then that new man wants a drink, and then . . ."

My foster father was an angry man: angry with America, angry with his work, angry with religion, angry with the Maels, angry with Helen, and often angry with me. The sole son-in-law, he found life within Helen's extended family stifling. By disposition less religious than they, he ridiculed their piety, labeling it hypocrisy. He mocked their religiosity to their faces, aggressively sitting down, for example, at those times in the service when the tradition required that all the men in shul stand.

Contributing in large measure to his anger, and Helen's embarrassment with him, was his failure in the world of work. The poultry business with Zayde and Uncle Eddy was never very profitable, but the vagaries of Saul's tantrums made it all the more difficult. An eye injury, caused by a snapping hook on the truck body used to secure the rope holding down the chicken crates, became the occasion for Saul to abandon the business and set off on his own. With great expectations he tried to buy a laundromat, week after week following newspaper leads in nearby towns. Nothing materialized. He spent several unsuccessful years as an itinerant salesman, an odd vocation for an awkward man so little likely to make pleasant small talk. I remember the large van in our driveway from which he tried to sell "coffee-time" drinks to grocery stores, which was replaced by another van from which he sold screws and bolts to hardware stores. This, too, an unlikely job for someone so utterly unhandy. Then he tried selling eggs, buying them in bulk from farmers, sorting them by size in our basement, and then delivering them to homeowners in the Boston suburbs. He was not the jolly egg-man, alas, and this enterprise didn't last long either.

After floundering like this for years he was finally given a job, a humiliating job, which he kept, lifting heavy bales of cotton some fifteen miles away in a textile mill in Dedham owned by a rich relative of the Maels, Benny Siegel. Saul hated the job as well as Benny, who paid all his workers, Saul included, the minimum wage, making it clear that if they made demands, he, too, might move to the Carolinas, as most New England mill owners were doing. Compounding the embarrassment for Helen of this litany of Saul's economic failures was the *shanda*, the shame, of his willingness to sell hardware or eggs, or even work at the mill, on the occasional Saturday.

We were never close. I was frightened by his temper, furious when he hit me, embarrassed by his antics in shul and driving on Shabbos, but, unlike Helen, I was not ashamed of his jobs. He was uninterested in me and seldom made an effort to do things with me, except to teach me to play the card games solitaire and casino. Unlike most immigrants and the Maels, he had never become interested in sports, one of my consuming passions. He seemed like a hermit to me, seldom leaving the house and even more rarely both-ering to talk to me or Helen, except to offer periodic denunciations of Zayde or one of my uncles. When he tried to relate to me it took the form of vulgar yiddishisms, delivered in a kind of "we men can share this" tone. "What time is it," he would ask; I would dutifully answer "half-past nine," which produced the inevitable rhyming punch line "kish mir in tuchos arein" (kiss my bottom). I have often wondered in my adult years what traces of Saul I bear other than wearing my watch, like he did, on the inside of my wrist. There is a bit of the crude Jewish joke teller in me, as well, and occasionally an inclination to run against the grain, to shock: for better with revi-sionist ideas, for worse with antisocial manners. And I enjoy too much pricking the pompous and the pious.

Early in my years in Millis I realized that the Spiros' marriage was deeply troubled. They fought constantly, each hurling Yiddish and Polish curses at the other, *fahbrent in drerd* (burn in hell), *paskunyak* (bitch/bastard), *galempta maladetz* (crippled dumbbell), and always the rejoinder, *gamatim* (the same to you). They made no effort to keep me from hearing the fighting, though I suppose they assumed the foreign languages would keep me from understanding. But who needed a translation? There was little affection between them. They knew exactly how to enrage each other. Helen simply had to mimic his foreign accent, "Vell, so vat big deal you done today? Ven vee going to see de money?" or accuse him of eating scallops on the road, and he just had to complain about the food she put in front of him, "Vatt is dis dreck?" (dirt), for pandemonium to break out. Plates flew to the floor; he might hit her, or she him, all in front of me. There could be a few tender moments, to be sure. When Saul felt affectionate, he sang her an Eddie Cantor song, "Barney Google (With the Goo-Goo-Googly Eyes)" and praised her pretty eyes. She, in turn, when feeling good about Saul, made him his favorite treat, fried egg and *tsibbeles* (onions), the smell of which thrilled me as a signal that a truce had taken effect. These cease-fires were all too temporary, alas, and each night before bed I repeated a prayer: "I hope and pray God that mommy and daddy will stop fighting and that there will be peace in the world," my own prescient Cold War blending of the public and private.

Bedtime was troubling enough for me without having to hear them yelling at each other downstairs, for I knew that several hours after I fell asleep Saul would go to bed not with Helen but with me. Through all my years in Millis, even in high school, we lived the public fiction that they shared a double bed in "their" mahogany bedroom and I had "my own" maple bedroom. What had begun as an accommodation to a scared five-year-old in 1943 became the modus operandi to a loveless marriage in both of our two-bedroom apartments and then in the two-bedroom house we moved to when I was thirteen. Whatever sense of security I may have derived from the arrangement as a child disappeared with distaste as we both grew bigger, I in years and Saul in girth. I slept motionlessly on the edge of the bed to avoid the slightest inadvertent contact with his body. It was, in fact, my room in all other respects. Saul's clothes and personal effects were in "their" bedroom. Only we three knew where he slept. I never complained; I didn't want to make trouble. I cannot, these years later, fathom how unpleasant this must have been throughout late childhood and adolescence, or even worse, how much I must have feared questioning it. Of course, I realize that immigrants in cramped tenements, and even today urban and rural poor, shared beds with many sleeping together, children with children, children with adults. It was just so unnecessary and selfish in my case.

Sometimes I did get to sleep alone. Very occasionally I woke up on a Sunday morning to find Saul's side of the bed empty and heard them together in Helen's room, down the hall. There were also periodic visits by Mr. Wells when Saul also slept with Helen. An accountant from New York City who kept the books for a mill in Medway, Mr. Wells was an Orthodox Jew who needed kosher meals, so he boarded with the Spiros for two or three days a month. This provided income for Helen, who also liked having this distinguished-looking professional man, in his nice suits, around the house, complimenting her cooking, even if it meant that for appearances' sake she had to share her bed with Saul on those nights. I had mixed feelings about these monthly visits. On the one hand, I had to give up "my" room altogether, since Mr. Wells took it over during his stay; on the other hand, it was apparent to me that my mother was more animated and less unhappy during his visits, and I also enjoyed that this important-seeming man actually inquired about my schoolwork and told me how bright he thought I was. And, of course, I treasured these opportunities to sleep alone, even if it was on the living room sofa. Not until I went off to college and came home on weekends and vacations did I find the courage to insist on my own bed. The state's visitors, of course, knew nothing about this bizarre sleeping arrangement, noting repeatedly "boy has his own room."

Helen had two passions: me and Hadassah. One consumed her formidable energy at home, the other outside the house. I had no sense, of course, as I was growing up that I owed some of the good fortune of her attention to and affection for me to her failed marriage. But I was very much aware of her tireless involvement with Hadassah, her other alternative to Saul.

Hadassah was America's most important women's Zionist organization. Founded in 1912 in New York City, its inspiration was the Baltimore-born Henrietta Szold, daughter of a rabbi, who was herself a distinguished journalist, scholar, and social worker. After a 1909 visit to Palestine, then a part of the Ottoman Empire, Szold committed herself to what she called "practical Zionism," by which she meant meeting the medical needs of Jews emigrating to the Holy Land. She called the first meeting of her group in 1912 on behalf of the "daughters of Zion," but the name was quickly changed to Hadassah, since the inaugural meeting coincided with the Jewish holiday Purim and Hadassah is the Hebrew name for Esther, the biblical heroine celebrated in the Purim story. Szold moved to Palestine permanently in 1920, when it came under the British Mandate, where she indefatigably established medical and nursing schools and child support agencies. Meanwhile, Hadassah flourished in America. By the 1940s local chapters across the country absorbed the energy of hundreds of thousands of Jewish women of all ages, as it does to this day.

Helen had little interest in the Zionist ideals of Henrietta Szold. Indeed, Orthodox Jews like the Maels assumed that the land of Israel would be re-created by the *Moshiach*, the Messiah, not secular Zionists or kibbutznik socialists. While no Zionist, Helen was preoccupied with *Yiddishkeit* (Jewishness). She had no close friends, but among her mere acquaintances there were no non-Jews. I grew up hearing that so-and-so in the newspaper or on television had "the map of Jerusalem on his face," or getting the count of how many Jews were among the victims in a plane crash.

Like Saul, Helen had no hobbies, no interests other than cooking. She didn't sew, knit, or read. She had little social life other than Hadassah, which for her meant involvement with middle-class Jewish women in the neighboring towns of Medway and Franklin in whom she saw her own social aspirations realized, women with successful businessmen husbands like Mrs. Garelick, married to the owner of a large milk and ice cream company (whose milk trucks are now seen all across New England); Mrs. Simon, married to the owner of a furniture store; and the wives of several Jewish doctors. Hadassah meant getting out of the house to meetings in other people's houses. Helen, who (unlike her sisters-in-law) could drive a car, journeyed to countless meetings, usually alone.

Saul hated Hadassah. The mere mention of her going to yet another meeting set him ranting almost as much as his disdain for her family, not that he ever needed to use the car in the evening. What particularly infuriated him was that Hadassah invaded the house as well. Helen knew better than to chance small meetings at her house, ever fearful of Saul being on display, but she did spend hours on the phone with Hadassah work. "Last year you took half a page in the Donor Dinner Book; can I put you down this year for a full page?" she asked one local businessman after another. "It only costs $5.00 to put your little David on our jewels' list," she'd tell a proud new grandmother. Meanwhile, people called her constantly to offer contributions, send Hadassah greeting cards, and plant trees in Israel, by way of noting births, deaths, and other family milestones. My mother had good organizational skills and was very successful in her Hadassah work, which brought her a lot of personal satisfaction and appreciative recognition from her colleagues. She would have been, I suspect, a successful professional person had she ever had the chance. She had a good sense of humor as well and was a fine mimic, and since Saul had a short fuse on this subject, I was the audience for her often hilarious accounts of her Hadassah life.

Helen loved to cook. She spent hours in the kitchen each day, often inefficiently, to be sure. Cooking relaxed her and passed the time. Like her Hadassah work, it provided an important part of her self-esteem. There was a competitive aspect to her cooking as well, as she boasted that she was a much better *balaboosta*, homemaker, than her *shvigas*, her sisters-in-law Becky and Esther, though she conceded that Nelly was very good. She always mocked the openly affectionate marriage of Eddy and Esther, who for so many of my childhood years had lived upstairs, but what particularly upset her was that her infatuated brother was, to her mind, blind to how bad a cook Esther was.

Every Friday Helen made boiled chicken and soup for Shabbos, though none of the three of us liked the white meat, which Helen fried as cutlets on Sunday. She was a wizard with sweet and sour stuffed cabbage and with cakes, cookies, and pies. Years later I made many a friend in college by sharing the strudel and blueberry squares from the care packages she sent me.

It's a shame that I did not appreciate these skills while I was growing up. Like most children, I had pedestrian taste buds and dreaded the supper table as the battlefield in the combat between my foster parents. Meals were unbearably tense. Helen put food in front of Saul first, hunched down over his plate; he would just about finish it before Helen, after giving me food, sat down herself. Saul insisted at every meal that I eat a piece of rye bread. "If you're hungry enough to eat, you need bread," he'd angrily offer as sacred folk wisdom. He never complimented my mother, and I didn't realize I might—or should. Instead, I usually sat there steeling myself for Saul's explosion. Only Helen visibly enjoyed and savored the food she had made, though she often contributed to the general tension by asking, if one of us had left food on the plate or turned down offers of more, "What's the matter, you don't like it?"

We had very little common family life beyond these meals. Each of the three places we lived in these years, the apartments on Village and Main Streets and the very nice two-floor house we moved into on Pleasant Street, which Zayde helped Helen buy in 1951, had nice living rooms, but we seldom sat in them. There were no books in the house, no news or general magazines like *Time* or *Life*, only

Helen's *Ladies' Home Journal, Redbook,* and *McCall's.* There was no music in the house, no record player, stereo, or hi-fi. We read newspapers, the *Boston Globe* and the *Milford News,* but we never talked about the news. We never listened to the radio together, except for the morning report of egg prices. We had a TV by about 1950, but we never watched it as a family. Hadassah and my homework came first. We never once in my childhood went to a movie together; it was yet another activity Saul hated. No one ever came to our house for dinner, and we were never invited to other people's houses for meals. The Spiros, it seemed, had no social life, and we ourselves seldom ate out as a family, though *oysessen* (eating out), to be sure, was rare for all Orthodox families in those years. I remember only one family vacation while living in Millis, a tense Christmas-week car ride to President Roosevelt's home and grave in Hyde Park along the Hudson, and then a snowy drive into New York City, where we stayed the night and had a rare meal at Lou Siegel's kosher restaurant on Thirty-Eighth Street. Helen went on her own to a Jewish hotel in Old Orchard Beach, Maine, in the summer of 1949, right after the eviction crisis.

None of these missing things bothered me at the time; life was good from my perspective. I went to the movies upstairs in the Medway Town Hall with friends on most Sunday afternoons for thirty-five cents. But true bliss was listening to the radio in "my" room before I fell asleep, except, of course, on Friday nights, when I couldn't use the radio. Like Woody Allen in his movie *Radio Days,* my sense of a world outside my rural shtetl came from radio. Who knew of water commissioners until hearing *The Great Gildersleeve,* of places called the Orient or Canada unless one listened to *The Shadow* and *Sergeant Preston?* My favorite distant place was Broadway, which I learned about from the program I most eagerly waited for each week, *The Railroad Hour.* When, on Mondays, Gordon MacRae sang an abbreviated version of an operetta by Victor Herbert or a musical by Rodgers and Hart, I heard my calling and saw my role in life. "Sing and dance on Broadway," I always told my friends every time we went around with what we wanted to do when we grew up. I never made it, alas, but I like to think there's a bit of an actor in all good teachers.

Close behind radio as a treat was the one thing my foster parents and I did as a family, take trips to Boston, which seemed like a foreign country to me. Helen and Saul seldom fought on the hourlong car ride, maybe because they were unable to see each other's eyes, which made it tougher to fan the other's anger. They sat up front, so I had the whole back seat of the Chevrolet to myself. Jews always drove General Motors cars in those days, never Fords. The anti-Semitic activism of Henry Ford was too raw in the memory of Jewish Americans. Throughout the 1920s, the industrialist's newspaper, *The Dearborn Independent*, insisted in a column entitled "The International Jew: The World's Problem" that there was a Jewish conspiracy to control the world, led by Jewish bankers who had brought about World War I. He also sponsored the publication and widespread distribution of the *Protocols of the Elders of Zion*, a forgery by tsarist secret police at the end of the nineteenth century purporting to be lectures by a "Jewish Elder" describing a Jewish plot to overthrow European governments and gain control of the world. Hitler would make much use of these bogus *Protocols*. Henry Ford died in 1947 convinced that Jewish bankers had caused World War II as well.

So it was, then, that we drove a Chevrolet on these glorious trips to Boston. Sometimes we went to the Jewish neighborhoods of Dorchester and Roxbury to buy new clothes, other times to pick up kosher meat or get the Pesach (Passover) order of "kosher for Passover" kosher food. These trips sometimes led to the rare *oyses-sen*: a sandwich at the fabled G&G Restaurant on Blue Hill Avenue in the heart of Jewish Boston, where Irish politicians from Mayor James Michael Curley (when he wasn't serving time in jail) to old John McCormack, the Speaker of the House, and young Jack Kennedy came to eat a pastrami or corned beef sandwich for a photo op for the *Boston Globe*, the *Boston Herald*, and, of course, the *Jewish Advocate*, greater Boston's English-language weekly Jewish newspaper.

In those years one of Massachusetts's most colorful political figures, Julius (Julie) Ansel, held perpetual court in the G&G Restaurant. Representing the Jews of Boston in the state legislature, he was a theatrical figure, fond of pompous oratory laced with Shakespeare. He was renowned for the not infrequent, but truly

artful, heart seizures in midspeech at the State House to win sym-
pathy for his issue followed a few hours later by a meal in his booth
at the G&G, where he charmed his constituents. I never encoun-
tered Julie Ansel at the G&G, but I remember vividly sitting in the
booth of the long-since-shuttered restaurant slowly savoring corned
beef on rye and pickle spears and drinking cream soda, a uniquely
peaceful and tension-free meal with Saul and Helen. It was heaven,
as was the ride home, with peaceful chatter drifting toward me from
the front seat.

We went to Boston for family visits, as well. On my mother's side
was the "cousins club," infrequent get-togethers of Bubby's Steinberg
relatives, to which only Helen and Saul among the Maels bothered
to go. Here I discovered a different American Jewry, which the great
Jewish writers like Malamud, Roth, and Bellow would explore. I
met relatives who weren't religious and others who were "communists," or so my foster parents labeled them because they had black
friends and played chess, the latter certifying them, in the parlance
of the 1950s, as "egghead" intellectuals. I was intrigued by what to
me was the exotic edge of my urban cousins, until at least the time
when, as the Cold War intensified, we decided it was too danger-
ous to see them.

The pleasure of Boston trips is most indelibly associated with a
relative on Saul's side, his uncle, the head of the Moshav Zikenim,
the Boston Hebrew Home for the Aged, who lived on the grounds
of the home, or the "hotel," as I called it. Jewish philanthropy, provided mainly by the successful first wave of German newcomers,
created communal institutions in American cities to look after sick,
orphaned, and elderly Jews, whose numbers swelled with the massive
wave of Eastern European immigration at the turn of the twentieth
century. Well-to-do Jews were proud to subsidize these charities,
vying to be on the boards of directors of the landmark institutions.
Just such a board of virtuous men and women in the 1930s chose
Saul's uncle, Morris Citron, a Polish Jew, to be resident director of its
imposing Hebrew Home for the Aged. For an impressionable ten-
year-old the visits were mystery and theater as dramatic and exciting
as any radio show. Somewhere in the Jewish part of Dorchester, our
Chevy turned off the busy street and went through heavy gates to

reappear on the grounds of the Home, presided over by Mr. Citron, as I called him. He lived in a small wing, set apart from the Victorian main building, with his two nieces, Eva and Brona, recently arrived, miraculously, from Poland. *Feta* (uncle) was a dour man with a large face topped by thick round glasses that almost hid his eyes. His every word announced his importance. His nieces were lovely, sophisticated young women with beautiful accents, who read books, went to the theater and concerts, and seemed like actresses to me.

We usually visited at mealtimes, which is probably why I called it the "hotel," and always ate in a private room at the end of the cavernous dining hall used by the residents. No matter how often we went I couldn't believe what I saw as we walked through the hall. Everyone was old, older even than Zayde and Bubby, and, of course, as Helen pointed out, there was a map of Jerusalem on every face as they turned to see who was eating with Mr. Citron. Sometimes uncle had other guests as well, often rich benefactors from the Boston community, yet another kind of Jew foreign to my Millis Jewish mentality but surely one of the reasons Helen enjoyed these visits. After eating and passing once again through the strange collection of elderly and invalid we returned to Mr. Citron's private quarters, with its outsized and overstuffed Jacobean furniture. While I hovered about picking up the paper rings, Saul, his uncle, and other male guests smoked Uncle's expensive cigars and played pinochle. Helen, the nieces, and any other women present talked about things I didn't understand, though I'm not sure, given her sometimes uncharacteristic silences, that Helen always did either. The lovely adventure always ended with me falling asleep in the Chevy's back seat, watching the lights of the passing cars and being carried from the car to bed an hour later.

Despite the day-to-day tensions in the Spiro house, despite everything, I was, by and large, a happy child in Millis. And so it was, in fact, in the Division of Child Guardianship visitors record: "he is happy in her home"; "child seems happy, well placed, and well cared for"; "he always seems happy." But my happy memories of growing up in Millis, trips to Boston, and playing with friends are seldom set inside the Spiros' house. Wherever I lived, downstairs on Village Street until I was eleven, above the shop near the town center for the next two years, or in the house on Pleasant Street, the indoors seemed gloomy and tense. Fun, as a boy, was outside the house and usually with my closest friend Gerry Nirenberg, who lived across Village Street in a large ramshackle house set back some distance from the road. We were inseparable, whether roaming across fields, playing ball, or staging cowboy and Indian showdowns in the trees that surrounded our houses. To play the enemy we sometimes enlisted my cousins from upstairs, Marilyn and Barbie, or Marty Viener, the chubby son of the man who owned our house, whom we never really liked, and whom we stopped asking to be an Indian after he hit me with an arrow in the corner of my eye. Gerry and I played outside every day in my elementary school years, exploring every pasture, stream, and wood within miles of our houses, parting only at dusk when we were expected home.

Gerry's family were not observant Jews and a bit shabby for Helen's taste, because his father was a delivery man and truck driver, in and out of work. She did admire Gerry's uncle, who had a prosperous ice cream business in Medway and whose wife sometimes went to Hadassah meetings. I was with Gerry when he heard that his uncle's twin daughters had fallen through the ice on a pond in Medway and drowned. We were doubly shocked because on that mild winter day Gerry and I had ourselves walked across the ice on the pond at the bottom of Village Street in Millis.

We were also together when our part of town was almost destroyed by fire. Gerry and I were ten and playing on a sunny summer day in a back pasture behind the Mael shul. After an hour or so rushing up and down fields pretending to be the American and German armies and falling dead on the ground innumerable times, we sat on a hilltop to smoke the cigarettes Gerry had taken from home. As we concentrated on enjoying our first cigarettes, it took a while to smell the burning grass one of our matches had set aflame. The fire had gone beyond our capacity to put out, and Gerry and I ran to our respective houses, acting as if nothing was amiss. Fortunately, someone had called the fire department and the trucks arrived in time to keep the flames from moving to the synagogue and houses. We told no one about what we had done and no one said anything to us, though I clutched at dinner that night when Helen remarked that it was unusual for me to have come home at midafternoon. I worried for a week that the firemen, or worse yet, the police, would seek me out. They didn't, and Gerry and I resumed our lazy bucolic summer explorations. But we never smoked again. I didn't ponder the moral implications of getting off scot-free. I sometimes wonder whether my adult professional interest in justice might not stem in part from a childhood experience of injustice, as it had for Jean-Jacques Rousseau. But Rousseau tells us in his *Confessions* that it was for being punished for something he hadn't done (steal a comb), whereas in my case it was for not being punished for something I did do.

Whether or not Helen suspected her son was an arsonist, she was often critical of my boyhood ways. She had high expectations and wanted me to be more mature and less irresponsible. When I was eleven, she complained that I went off to play with Gerry instead of staying home to meet the social worker. "Sonny does not seem to grow up," she observed. "For someone who gets good grades in school," she wondered, "why isn't he more serious in his play?" I was, she reported, a "bit cocky" at home, "uninterested in telling her much about school" and "very inconsiderate in small things." Turns out she had trouble getting me to wear my rubbers and rain-coat on rainy days and to eat all of my lunch. Apparently, the social worker had heard one too many complaints, noting that "Sonny has a desire to emancipate himself from such rigid parental supervision," which may well be one reason I so loved the freedom of playing outside the house and in the fields. But what neither Helen nor the social worker knew was that cocky, insubordinate Sonny sometimes donned his rubbers when he left the house for school and then rebelliously hid them behind a tree near the school bus stop, thankfully still a full eleven hundred feet from the house. At the end of the day, Sonny got off the school bus, put them back on, and marched home. No one was the worse for it.

CHAPTER 5

Yiddishkeit
and Baseball

My errant ways notwithstanding, my emerging sense of self was very much being shaped by the moral universe of *Yiddishkeit* (Jewishness). It was all-consuming, structuring my experience of everyday life, defining the rhythm of each day, week, and year. Jewishness gave me a foundational identity, a strong feel for who I was. I was Jewish not merely in a cultural or historical sense but in a fundamental, religious way.

The Mael family's orthodoxy was grounded not in a particular doctrinal perspective but in the simple belief that the good Jew performed the hundreds of biblical requirements of prayer and abided by all the commandments regulating food, work, and rest. I shared the Maels' assumption that the Orthodox Jew whose life was governed by these obligatory rituals of *frumkeit* (piety) was a morally superior being, better than the nonobservant Jew, the non-*shab-bostiche* (non–Shabbos observer), and certainly more worthy than *goyim* (non-Jewish people). Like the seventeenth-century Puritans, the Maels saw themselves on "an errand in the wilderness," bearing witness in twentieth-century rural Massachusetts to the true faith by meticulously living the law of the Old Testament God.

To a small boy, being Jewish meant being *mirturnisht* (forbidden) to do certain things. And the Maels had a much larger list of things *mirturnisht* than others. While most of Millis's Jews did not eat *treyf*, the proscribed bacon, pork, and shellfish, or mix meat with dairy, only the Maels waited a full six hours after eating meat before eating dairy products. While others had a *mezuzah*—a small wooden or metal container with holy words on parchment inside, attached to the side of the door frame on their front doors, which they touched with kissed fingers on entering and leaving—only the Maels had one on every doorway in the house. Only the Maels never worked, never drove, never carried anything, never put on a light or an appliance, never wrote, and never answered the phone from Friday evening to Saturday evening and on religious festivals. Only the Maels prayed every morning and every evening at home and every Shabbos in their own shul. They took great pride in this distinction and the knowledge that many Jews in the Boston area knew of the Maels' righteousness on their farm out in the country.

The repetitive routines of Jewish ritual anchored my life. Every morning (except Shabbos) for about four years, before and after my bar mitzvah at age thirteen, I "lay tefillin." Winding thin pieces of black leather around my skinny left arm, wrist, and fingers, I chanted the morning prayers, usually with the swaying back and forth motion I saw my elders use in shul. That I couldn't understand a word of what I was saying, or what I recited in synagogue, since I could read Hebrew but not translate it, captures the quality of my religiosity. The fine points of spiritual dogma—comprehending doctrine, exploring meaning, or affirming faith—were irrelevant; being a religious Jew for me meant performing the rituals and reciting the prayers God had commanded, and not doing that which was *mirturnisht*.

It was a *shanda*, a shameful transgression, to do what was forbidden, like eating meat and dairy products at the same meal. Since God worried that an animal might be eaten along with the milk of its mother, the bread one ate with chicken or beef could not be buttered. The Maels and the Spiros had four sets of dishes, silver-ware, and pots, two large sets for meat and dairy, two smaller sets used just during the Passover Week. There were also a few special dishes set aside for the occasional non-Jewish eater, like the painter Rufus, who might eat a meal when working for them.

A newspaper would be put on the table and Rufus, who never seemed to have a last name, would eat his sandwiches, perhaps ham, on dishes reserved for *treyf*, nonkosher, food. I learned to read Hebrew in the Hebrew school where I studied from the age of ten until my bar mitzvah. Two hours a day, four afternoons a week, I joined four other boys at the other shul where Mr. Siegel, the owner of Cohen's Hotel, was the *melamed* (teacher) in what was less a school than an old-fashioned shtetl *cheder*, a religious train-ing academy. We spent two years learning to read Hebrew by rote memorization and a third learning to recite and sing our particu-lar bar mitzvah portions of the Torah. We learned no Jewish history and nothing about holidays and festivals. There was nothing cozy or warm about Hebrew school. The *cheder* was as tyrannical as any in the old country, with Mr. Siegel bullying us with shouted rep-rimands and the occasional brutal slap. A large man whose blows stung, he was an indifferent teacher who went through the motions for the little extra money the job provided, since Cohen's Hotel, which he bought after a failed legal career in Trenton, New Jersey, was the most marginal of the four Jewish hotels in town. He was the first streetwise urban Jew I met, but what fascinated me most about him were his attractive daughters, who were my age and seemed much more sophisticated than girls who grew up in Millis. These daughters loomed much larger in our thoughts than his perfunc-tory and painful pedagogy. In any event, what little respect we had for our teacher disappeared one day after school when he overheard us exchanging body-parts jokes and assured us that our "privates" were used only to go to the toilet.

Though we thought him a fool, he did what he was paid to do: he prepared us for our bar mitzvahs and pretty much wrote the lit-tle speeches we made interpreting the Torah portions we had read and thanking our parents for "all they had done to make this won-derful day possible." I threw myself into the yearlong preparation

for reciting my *haftorah*, the Hebrew prophetic passage connected
to that week's Torah text, not from any spiritual commitment but
more from my longing for a career on the stage. I liked to sing and
found the cadences of the traditional rhythms pleasing. Nor did I
mind being the center of attention. When my bar mitzvah Shabbos
came in March 1951, I knew it was a special day because my cousin
Teddy, the son of Mark, the one Mael brother who didn't live in
Millis, came to stay with us—the first time anyone my age had slept
at my house—and also because all the women in the family came
to shul, unlike a typical Shabbos. I did fine that day, and my pres-
ents enabled me to deposit $200 in my first bank account. After the
service we all went across the street to Nelly's dining room for the
celebratory kiddush, at which Saul, to my relief, did not get drunk.

Much of the enveloping warmth and pleasure that Judaism provided me as a boy I associate with the Mael shul and Nelly's house.
The shul had two sanctuaries, and most of the time we *davened*
(prayed) in the smaller one, a long narrow room about ten feet
wide on the western side of the building, which one had to walk
through to get into the larger shul. A long bench ran along each
of the walls, except for where the reader's lectern and a small *aron
kodesh* (a recessed cabinet for the Torah, covered with a decorative
curtain) stood on the inner eastern wall, which separated this shul
from the larger one. No more than fifteen or twenty men could sit
in this plain, unadorned space, which sufficed for Shabbos services
all winter. The larger sanctuary, about one hundred feet square, was
used on Shabbos in the summer and on the High Holidays, when
hotel Jews and Mael family women came to services. It had hard
benches facing east, a large raised *bimah* (the reader's table), several chairs on a walk-up platform in the middle of the shul, and
a larger *aron kodesh* holding several Torahs in the middle of the
eastern wall, which one walked up several steps to open and close.
The small women's gallery, built above the small sanctuary, ran the
length of the western side. The simple severity of the room was broken only by the bright red embroidered coverlet on the *bimah* table
and the bright red curtain enclosing the *aron kodesh*. There were
large round top windows on three sides, through which one could
see Zayde's house across the field and Nelly and Harry's across the

street. In the shul's dark and dank basement was a toilet used only by the hotel visitors, since the rest of us preferred to walk to Nelly's.

Shabbos services were led by Zayde or Harry, his oldest son, though most of the time anarchic autonomy seemed to reign as men swayed their heads and upper bodies, *davening* in Hebrew, at their own pace and in their own private worlds. Walking around, chatting, and strolling in and out of shul were not uncommon. Still, at a moment during the *Amidah*, a long continuous set of prayers near the end of the service, or at the reading of the Torah, the minyan became as one, standing, sitting, and reciting in unison. I swayed and I *davened*, having no idea what I was saying—Orthodox *sidorim* (prayer books) did not provide an English translation—caught up in the intoxicating shared communal experience that most of the year was indistinguishable from a family ritual, since everyone was family, my family. Only a nagging fear that Saul would act up disturbed my pleasure. When we prayed in the large shul, he might sit by himself in the small shul for what seemed like hours to me. Even worse, when Zayde, Uncle Harry, and the other men reverently stood, he often remained seated.

I had another recurring fear in shul. When the Torah was read I worried I would be given an *aliyah*, the honor of being called to the *bimah* to stand witness to part of that week's reading. No one in the Mael shul read the *brachah*, the short blessings that preceded and followed the reading; everyone knew them by heart. In the winter, especially, when there was usually just a minyan, the mathematics was daunting, with odds of seven out of ten that I'd be called. I repeated the prayers over and over under my breath as I heard Zayde call up each *aliyah* in turn. When called I usually performed flawlessly, but to this day when I venture into a synagogue I get tense at Torah reading time, fearing for some strange reason that this will be the day I get an *aliyah*, and rehearse the *brachah* to myself in anticipation. As an adult, I often dream that I am in shul sitting without a *yarmulka*, the required skullcap, sometimes wearing only underwear, a rebuke in my subconscious, I suppose, for abandoning my religiosity, so wrapped up as it is with nostalgic memories of childhood and family.

I liked the theater of our little shul, especially at holidays. Zayde was a born performer, a master of the dramatic. Each Rosh Chodesh (the turn of the month) we walked outside the shul and prayed in the dark to the new moon. On Purim, Zayde staged the *Megillah*, the story of Esther, like a biblical soap opera. Distributing wooden *gragars*, noise makers, to everyone, he led a raucous cacophony at every mention of the wicked Haman. When the heroic Esther was named, he urged sweet sighs of approval. On the fall holiday of Sukkot, Zayde shook the *esrog* (citron) and *lulav* (palm frond) in all directions with a somber authority, looking like a stern Old Testament tribal priest plunked down in a Millis pasture. On Simchas Torah, the fall celebration of the Torah, a different Zayde, an Eastern European mystic, joyfully sang and danced in frenzied abandon, lost in trance-like encounters with his God.

Zayde was at his best on the High Holidays of Rosh Hashonah and Yom Kippur, when his audience was augmented by the hotel crowd, and it is these "days of awe" I most vividly remember. Like everyone else, I arrived for services wearing new clothes, as much a New Year's *yontif* (holiday ritual) as eating apples and a slice of round challah with honey at Rosh Hashonah dinner. I had no idea, of course, of the hard bargaining between Helen and the state that produced my outfit. On the High Holidays Zayde wore a *kittel*, a special long white smock, over his suit, kept secure by a white band tied at his waist, meant to evoke the white burial shroud placed on the Jewish dead. Over the *kittel* he wore his *tallis*, prayer shawl, and on his head was a special raised white *yarmulka* that looked to me like a shortened chef's hat. Most unusual were the white tennis shoes he and my uncles wore. Wearing leather on these special days of penance was prohibited. Zayde did everything: he led the service, blew the *shofar*, the ram's horn, and read the Torah. Enthusiastically and lightheartedly, he coaxed money for charity and the shul from family and visitors by auctioning off *aliyahs* and the opportunity to open the Torah ark during the service. At dramatic parts of the service, he sobbed with remorse and punctuated his cries by banging his right fist against his heart.

The Torah reading for the first day of Rosh Hashonah is about the sacrifice of Isaac. While I couldn't translate the text as Zayde chanted it, I knew the story. I realized full well it had a happy ending, as the angel of God arrived just in time to substitute a passing ram for the little boy. But I could never free myself from the fear the reading provoked. Years later the story still troubles me. How could a just and loving God demand such a horrible sacrifice? My discomfort then was not rooted in theological doubt; it was one of the few times I experienced consciously the pain of a seemingly unloved Isaac whose father could decide to abandon him. Though I had no basis for it, I always believed that as Zayde intoned the story, year after year, he thought of me and saw himself as the angel of God who had helped bring me to Millis. My step outside the defensive shell in which I hid from thoughts of self was fleeting. Soon I was caught up again with the rituals of Rosh Hashonah, as Zayde blew the shofar with his long *tikiyoh gidoloh*, one of the prescribed notes, and with *tashlich*, when we walked from shul and cast our sins into the brook that ran through Zayde's field.

Fasting on Yom Kippur, the Day of Atonement, was easy for me, and I proudly began when I was ten. My foster parents and I ate our chicken dinner late in the afternoon on erev Yom Kippur, the evening before Yom Kippur, and walked to shul for the solemn Kol Nidre service. When we got there, the men, wearing *talleisim* the only evening all year they did, circulated around the big shul in what seemed like an elaborate ballet, asking each other to forgive any word or deed during the previous year that had been hurtful or offensive. The shul's three Torah scrolls were then brought to the *bimah*, held by Zayde's three sons, who, like him, wore white *kittels*, while Zayde chanted the Kol Nidre prayer three times, with the rest of us quietly joining in for the mournful opening phrase.

On Yom Kippur day itself, Zayde was at his charismatic best. He moaned, cried, trembled, and pleaded with God. He fell flat on the *bimah* floor, in sobbing subservience, then jumped up defiantly, proclaiming that giving charity, *tzedokah*, could inscribe everyone with a favorable verdict in God's book of life. When the service reached the archaic biblical list of calamities that would beset the unjust among us, "who will die of stoning, who of plague, who of hail," he hit his breast with a force that any self-flagellating Christian or Hindu might envy. His Yom Kippur sermon was always the same, delivered in a Yiddish I could easily follow. He said he was our lawyer pleading our case to God, the judge, who would decide that day

Fig. 8 | Isaac with the Mael cousins and Uncle Eddie

who would live and who would die in the next year. After a slow and
somber warning that he could only do so much for us, he loudly
and joyously declared that God would let the righteous, repentant,
and charitable among us live. When he finished the service, Zayde
was drained, covered with sweat, and physically shaking as we all
surrounded him, shouting *yashakech* (good job, well done). That
we knew every gesture, every flourish and inflection, from the year
before was no matter; we were mesmerized by his spiritual and emotional fervor. Only when we gathered in Nelly's dining room after
the *Neilah* (the concluding service) for the family dairy breakfast
meal was the spell finally broken.

　　Nelly's house, across the street, was virtually an extension of the
shul, and it, too, is indelibly associated with the warm and pleasur-
able reach of Judaism in my boyhood. After we moved from Village
Street to the center of Millis, I walked the two miles to shul on
Saturday morning and stayed at Nelly's the rest of the day. I looked
forward to Saturday and was proud that I was often needed after my
bar mitzvah to complete the minyan of ten, the minimum number

Fig. 9 | Isaac (*right front*) with the Mael grandchildren seated around Joseph and Etta Mael

necessary for a service. Sometimes, days of true bliss, I was driven to Nelly's on Friday afternoon and stayed until Saturday night.

Nelly, Harry, and their seven children lived downstairs in a large brown wooden house where Morris and Becky lived upstairs with their four children. These eleven cousins, five to ten years older than I, accepted me totally, as did my four other Millis cousins, Eddy and Esther's girls. With one exception, who went to Brandeis, my older Mael cousins went from high school into the cow business. Friendly and open, my "cousins" took a shine to me as soon as I arrived, and I had a warm relationship with all of them. They were provincial, conservative, Republican, and anti-intellectual, as, of course, was I, but they were decent, good people, except when they encouraged Saul to drink too much at kiddush. As the older cousins married, exotica infiltrated their ranks, albeit still religious. Phil Cohen was a Democrat and New Yorker; Leon Jacobs, a doctor from Quincy who moonlighted as a medic at auto races in New Hampshire; and

Estie Namier, a beautiful young woman from Montreal, a distant relative of Mordecai Richler, the Canadian novelist, who said her friends in Canada asked her how big the Mael ranch was.

Teeming with cousins, the house across the street from the shul seemed to be a happy house, pulsating with life and energy. During the week, it was the focus of the business. The cow barn for many years was right next door, ultimately replaced by a parking lot for the trucks and the Maels' gas pump. On Shabbos the downstairs was the extended family's community space with Nelly, its moral center, waiting on all of us. Nelly was the mother that books described. She was kind, gentle, noncomplaining, nonjudgmental, warm, and loving. No matter what she was doing, she always had time for me, time to find a crisp piece of *grieven*—fried and hardened chunks of chicken fat, the Jewish bacon. Knowing how much I cherished my visits there, she probably engineered a few. Everyone liked Nelly. She took in Zayde when Bubby died and looked after him in his declining years. She made room overnight for the bearded *meshulachim* (traveling charity collectors) who came periodically from Boston to pick up the *pushkes* (little tin charity boxes) in which Jews put money for yeshivas and orphanages. Above all, Nelly was a *balaboosta*—a housewife extraordinaire.

Some days she made doughnuts and let me drop the batter into the pot of boiling oil. I was not much taller than the dining room table on which she rolled and cut the noodles for the sweet *lockshen kugel* pudding I loved. She braided the dough for the challah she baked every week and hacked the carp in her brown wooden bowl for gefilte fish. Sweet carrot tzimmes and the slowly roasting cholent, the thick potato and meat dish that had been sitting in a *topp* (pot), cooked on the oil stove on Shabbos. Most of all, I remember Nelly's pinwheel cookies, crisp little round cinnamon and dough circles, no larger than a silver dollar, which magically materialized whenever I was there.

Sometimes I arrived at Nelly's early enough on Friday to see the newspapers underfoot, set out to cover the recently washed kitchen floor until Shabbos. After the chaos of everyone dashing about, washing and changing clothes, came the quiet moment when Nelly *bentch licht*—lit the Shabbos candles. Her head covered, she circled her arms and put them over her eyes and said the *brachah* (blessing). After the men *davened* in shul, we ate Nelly's chicken dinner, always chicken. Everybody fussed over me when I stayed at Nelly's; in the afternoon my older boy cousins allowed me to join their softball game on the hilltop pasture, though I never understood why this was allowed on Shabbos. With *havdalah*, the candle and incense ceremony held at Nelly's home that ended the Shabbos, I was always a little sad, even though I liked the sour cream and bananas that Nelly set out for us, for it meant I had to return to Helen and Saul's.

Nelly presided over all the *yontif* eating as well. The *sukkah*, the temporary shed covered with pine branches in which we ate during the festival of Sukkot, was built outside a window of her kitchen. On Chanukah we gathered in her dining room for potato latkes, which we ate with salt, not sour cream or apple sauce. And our Passover seders were held at an extended table that went through her dining room into the adjacent sun porch. All her kitchen counters were covered with boards and brown paper to block the surfaces where *chometz* (bread) had been the rest of the year. Zayde had a special chair at the seder, full of pillows, on which he lay back and relaxed, for on that night he represented us all, free Jews. On both sides of the long table sat his children, daughters-in-law, son-in-law, grandchildren, a few new spouses, and me. We read every word in the Haggadah and sang every song, always led by Zayde. Nelly opened the front door to welcome Elijah the prophet, and I, the youngest, asked the Four Questions, which I mastered by heart in Hebrew, Yiddish, and English.

Not that our seders were always peaceful. Frequently there was tension between upstairs and downstairs in the big house. Morris, from upstairs, caretaker of the money side of the cow business, could be counted on for a sarcastic aside. Saul was unpredictable. Even Zayde could tense up the table with complaints or pontifications. Once at the end of the seder meal, he launched into a tirade in Yiddish against his backsliding, *goyische* grandchildren because one of them, he had heard, while still coming to services at the Mael shul, had also joined the other shul (for social reasons) into which no Mael should step a foot. No one dared laugh as he ended his diatribe by muttering into his beard "and also the matzah balls tonight are too hard." If only to spare Nelly more unjustified calumny, some of us changed the subject to the Red Sox and the beginning of the baseball season, one of the few things about which Zayde had no opinions, since he and Saul were the only men in the family uninterested in baseball.

Baseball was my other foundational interest as I grew up, alongside Jewishness, and the two invariably met most years at Rosh Hashonah or Yom Kippur services when my cousins and I talked less about our fate in the "Book of Life" than about the World Series game we weren't allowed to listen to. I got hooked on baseball when I was eight. I know now that lots of middle-aged male writers become teary-eyed as they recall baseball's hold on their childhood, enlisting metaphors of youth, greenness, and time standing still in our only untimed sport, and I plead guilty to these clichés. But the truth is that I talked ceaselessly about baseball, played it, listened to it on the radio, and, most miraculously, watched it, since I was convinced TV was invented so that we could see Fenway Park.

I merged *Yiddishkeit* and baseball in ways that went beyond High Holiday conversations with cousins. I knew all about that rare species, the Jewish baseball player. I could recite in great detail the heroic feats of "Hammerin Hank" Greenberg, the slugger for the Detroit Tigers in the 1930s and 1940s, the first Jewish superstar in American sports. I was particularly proud that the year he hit fifty-eight home runs was the year I was born, 1938, and even prouder that he had refused to play on Yom Kippur in 1934, when the Tigers were in a hot pennant race. Closer to home, I knew all about the much less distinguished baseball career of Morris "Moe" Berg, the second-string catcher for the Boston Red Sox from 1935 to 1939. He was never a great player, but he was Jewish, a "magna cum laude" graduate of Princeton, and considered then to be America's "most scholarly professional athlete." He even appeared on the radio quiz show *Information Please*. What I didn't know was that Berg became a spy in World War II for the OSS, the Office of Strategic Services, and later for its successor, the CIA.

My friends and I talked incessantly about baseball; it was our conversational currency, since few of us listened to the same radio shows. Even in the winter we talked of trades on "the hot stove

league." In spring and summer we played baseball on Labointe's pasture on Pleasant Street, the most level field we could find. I always
pitched, assuming that then my poor hitting would be less noticed.
I learned from the radio, my first guide to baseball, that pitchers
never hit well. A night game won over all my weekly programs in
the summer, even *The Railroad Hour.* The "gee whiz" voice of the
announcer excitedly describing a home run, a double play, or a routine pop out filled my room with a cozy embrace even when he read
his description from the delayed teletype for games on the road.
Television announcers, I discovered, were more laconic because the
cameras automatically conveyed the drama and beauty of baseball
to awestruck viewers.

Repeated notations in my file contained social workers testifying
to my obsession: "Isaac talked about baseball . . . friendly outgoing
personality who has an avid interest in baseball . . . told visitor of
his activity in baseball of which he is very fond . . . hoping to play
baseball soon. . . . He talked about playing baseball and listening to
the Big League games. He is very much interested in the Red Sox
and is quite a follower of all Big League baseball."

I was not an indiscriminate fan, having one and only one love
affair, faithful always to the Red Sox. While Boston had the Braves
as well, I never cared for them, even in 1948 when they won the
National League pennant with the indomitable pitching rotation
of "Warren Spahn, Johny Sain, and pray for rain." I was obviously
not alone, for soon the Braves, for lack of fans, would leave Boston
for Milwaukee. My sacred ground was beautiful Fenway Park with
its left field wall, "the green monster." A few times I went to a night
game at Fenway with Uncle Eddy or an older cousin, never with
Saul. On the day of the game I worried about rain from the minute
I woke to the minute we came through the stadium tunnel and saw
the electrifying green of the outfield grass and the dazzling white
and red of the uniforms.

Only as the batting order was announced with the immortal
names "Dom DiMaggio, Johnny Pesky, Ted Williams, Vern Stephens,
Bobby Doerr" did I relax and chant with the rest of the crowd:
"Who's better than his brother Joe? Dominick DiMaggio." I loved
the Red Sox, alas, an unrequited love, which I've only given up in

recent years, but my heart really belonged to just one of them, Ted Williams, my only childhood hero. I worshiped him with a primal unwavering ardor, unlike many Red Sox fans who hated him even as they adored him. I was never upset by his spoiled-kid antics: yelling back at the crowd when they booed him, giving fans the finger or spitting at the left-field stands. Nor did my affection waver when he angrily threw his bat, which unfortunately hit a woman sitting behind the Red Sox dugout. He was perfection, the greatest hitter in baseball. He could do no wrong.

I knew everything about him. I knew he was named after Teddy Roosevelt, alongside whom his father had charged up San Juan Hill. I knew he had had a troubled childhood in San Diego, with a deeply religious Hispanic mother active in the Salvation Army and a roving father who eventually deserted his family. I knew that my idol had a brother who was in and out of trouble with the law. I knew that Ted, "the Kid," as writers referred to him, never wore ties at fancy dinners. I knew he gave four and a half years of his extraordinary career to the Air Force in World War II and Korea. I also knew that in 1941, when he won the batting title with the astounding average of .406, the last time anyone has hit over four hundred, he chose to play the last day of the season instead of preserving his average and raised it six more points that day. And I knew he was too proud to poke hits to left field through the infield after Lou Boudreau, the player manager of the Cleveland Indians, invented the "Williams Shift," in which he positioned the shortstop on the right side of second base. Williams was my hero even in my dreams. One night when my foster parents returned late from a visit to Nelly and Harry, they found me sleeping with the radio still on. When they turned it off, I awakened. The asked if anyone had called while they were out. "Yes," I answered groggily. "Ted Williams."

Williams was like Saul in a way—ornery, unconventional, embarrassing, and discourteous—but unlike Saul, he did wondrous things, like hitting over five hundred towering home runs even as he told people off, getting hits four out of every ten at bats in 1941, the very year he feuded with Boston sports writers.

But there is a downside to my worship of Williams that strikes a chord with my past: he and the Red Sox always let me down. Like so many others, I have been cursed with the misery that afflicts Sox fans. Forged in 1946, the year I discovered them, when St. Louis Cardinal Enos Slaughter hustled home from first base to score on a single, stealing the World Series from us, a deep pessimism haunts all Red Sox fans. We know that evil, usually taking the (almost) human form of the New York Yankees, always triumphs in life, and the good are doomed in an imperfect and unjust world. This, we know, is nature's law: no matter how well things seem to be going, the Sox will blow it. They can have a thirteen-game lead in August and lose the pennant; they can begin uncorking champagne in the locker room even as Billy Buckner lets the ball and the World Series slip through his legs. In baseball and in life, it's best to trust no one; they won't love you back, and they always let you down. Even Ted Williams, I now know, could not trust his children, one of whom has put his father's dead body headfirst in an Arizona deep-freeze facility, anticipating his return to life. Such an indignity, such a *shanda* for my hero. Unaffected in my youth by such moral musings, I tried out for the school team. I didn't know you got on simply by showing up. Taking one look at my skinny frame, the coach agreed that I would pitch. He knew our star pitcher, George Harris, whose father owned the gas station near the intersection of Main and Exchange, was strong enough to start every game. Anyway, I didn't stay on the team because most games were played on Saturday, which was clearly a "different ballgame" than softball with the cousins on Shabbos in the Mael pasture. Still, I've lived off the magical three weeks on the team all my life, with memories of "suiting up," jock strap, gray uniform, cleats, and occasionally pitching batting practice to save George's arm. The closest I've come to a team since is pitching for our faculty–graduate student softball team.

On the big baseball weekend of Memorial Day 1952, a little over a year after my bar mitzvah, I was getting a glass of milk in the kitchen before a pick-up game of baseball when I saw a penny postcard on the counter, an unusual place for mail, with its message side up. The card was from Max to Helen, and it had a short message. "Please tell Isaac that his mother died." I don't remember if I knew then that I had a living "real" mother or that she was "in a hospital." If I did, it was never on my mind. The subject was certainly not talked about, hence the postcard left for me to read. Max was reality, to be sure, with his dreaded visits every few months, but I was "Sonny," a Spiro and a Mael. I read the postcard, drank my milk, and went out to play baseball. Several months later, her death prompted my visitor to raise the topic of family with me. I don't remember this, but I have the file to record the moment.

The boy was seen privately on 9/16 and at that time we discussed with him his knowledge of his family background. He stated that he knew nothing of his family background and furthermore was not interested. He has had occasional visits from his father, one in April and one in August of this year, and on one occasion has met his brother Sigmund. In discussing his family he showed no signs of emotional feelings and in view of the fact that he stated he is not interested in knowing anything about his family we did not pursue this discussion any further.

Many years later, of course, I did become deeply interested in knowing anything about my family, especially about my real mother, the only one of the five Kramnicks I never met. I obtained her state records and at the age of forty saw my first image of her, the file photo: a serious, fleshy, round-faced, slightly angry-looking woman with glasses and short dark hair. I read the minimal notes recorded on those rare occasions when someone examined her in the last few of her fifteen years on the ward in Danvers State Hospital.

December 27, 1945: The patient was quite cooperative and seemed contented to stay in the hospital. The patient was not sad or depressed but seemed quite euphoric. Most of patient's answers to questions were of one word. She continually said that she wished to go to Ward B-1. Her voice was very indistinct making it difficult to understand what she was rambling on about. The patient said that she has been here for six years. At all times she was very unattentive. Questions had to be continually repeated before getting her attention. She hears voices which call her names.

February 26, 1948: Unimproved. Assumes flirtatious manners, has bright red lips and face rouge. Attentive, neat and cooperative. Rambling. Silly expression. Appears euphoric during interview.

States husband and children are on her mind. She wishes to be with them. Voices are "troublemakers" but she will not explain. She is in the hospital because her husband is "crazy, fired from working."

August 3, 1950: Unimproved attitude and manner. Patient is unusually destructive. Fairly neat, clean and tidy. Depressed and unhappy. Well developed and very poorly nourished white female.

In 1951, described as eating poorly and "losing considerable weight," Sarah was "placed on the D.L. because of malnutrition." That fall she was discovered to be "seriously ill with pulmonary T.B.," and in late May she died in the TB pavilion. "The body was claimed by her husband, Max, who made arrangement to send an undertaker." Two days later I read the penny postcard from Max to Helen.

I knew nothing of Leon's life in these Millis years, but he will return to my story, as will Sigmund. Neither concerned me in that bucolic boyhood of baseball and *Yiddishkeit*.

CHAPTER 6

The Millis Consolidated School

I never became a school athlete; it wasn't a Jewish thing. Still, I associate school with fun and success. The excitement began with the bus ride that took me immediately out of the gloom that hung over the Spiro house. As the bus meandered through the deeply rural Rockville part of town toward the Millis Consolidated School, the single building in the town center that contained all twelve grades, I chatted about baseball or politics with the farm boys who sat near me. One schoolmate, Alex Kubacki, remains immortalized in our collective memory for the afternoon the bus hadn't quite made it back to his farm when nature called. That virtually everyone in school knew the next day of his misfortune speaks volumes not only to childhood toilet obsessions and cruelty but to the school's small and tight knit community. After the Sharon Sanatorium I went through school, year after year, with the same twenty kids in my class. By high school I knew every one of the ninety or so boys and girls in the back wing of the building where grades nine through twelve were housed.

My class of twenty was not your typical swamp-Yankeeland crowd. There were two other Jews, my closest friend Gerry Nirenberg and my upstairs cousin Marilyn Mael, and two Armenians, Olga Maranjian and Ann Dederian. Most of us came from lower-middle-class environments; none of our parents had gone to college. We remained an amazingly stable group through all the grades, though our numbers were reduced to nineteen the week before graduation when Dick Pixley, the coolest of us all, died in a car crash, our rude initiation to the capricious world outside our brick school. And it was a place in which I thrived, according to the state visitors, who were obliged to visit the school each time they came to Millis. Their notations in my file chronicle their pride in my success and theirs in their successful placement. Miss Hargon, my third-grade teacher in 1946, told the visitor of me that "he always seems happy."

Mrs. Fernald, my fourth-grade teacher, reported the next year that "Isaac is a splendid student. If the child has any difficulty it is caused by his over conscientious attitude . . . says the child seems happy, well placed and well cared for." The social worker added a prescient observation: "Fourth grader Isaac continues to be tall and very thin. He created the impression of being fragile. He looks like a scholar."

The following spring, Mr. Brown, my ally in the "bus war" who would be the principal all my years in Millis Consolidated School, declared, "Isaac is an A student. He is a very nice child and very bright." Not as concerned with my appearance as the visitor, he also suggested that I was "slightly over-conscientious." In 1948 a visitor recounted a conversation with me in the schoolyard: "The boy has a courteous manner and attractive personality. He apparently is an excellent student in school. He said he received A and A+ in his school report." Referring to the Spiros, the visitor wrote, "The boy seems to have every advantage that it is possible to have."

By the time I was ten, school visits produced meticulously detailed official grades for my file in reading, spelling, arithmetic, history, and even hygiene. All were As, with solid Bs in handwriting and drawing. The social worker comments, "It seems advisable to record this report card for future reference since boy is undoubtedly college material."

In 1949, in seventh grade, my first year in junior high school, I was transferred to the Division of Child Guardianship's Division of Older Boys, and to a new visitor, who described me as "neatly dressed, the youngest one in his class, a rather underweight boy with an alert intelligent look." Having learned that I was on the honor roll and received mainly As, the "visitor praised Isaac for his achievement and the boy smiled rather self-consciously." This visitor went beyond mere praise, apprising me of what would prove to be one of the state's most beneficent interventions. "Visitor told Isaac that if he applied himself and showed interest and the desire to proceed with further education, this Dept. might be able to assist him. Isaac talked about sports."

As proud as my visitors were of my achievement, and convinced as they were that this was an unusual foster care story, my foster mother's sense of me was more complicated. Her foster parent reports, parts of which were quoted in the file, reveal an intense pride in my religiosity and in my grades, with the implication, not without merit, that the home she was providing accounted for "his achievement." "The Division," she wrote, "doesn't appreciate what I have done for Sonny, to make him what he is. It never tells me that I am an unusual foster mother." But she found fault in me, as well. When I was twelve she noted, "Isaac used to want to be with foster parents at all times. Now, he is showing a tendency to want to be more with his friends." Complaining here of what another might see as normal maturation, Helen also referred to what she views as my stunted development. "Foster mother made the comment that Isaac did not seem to grow up." She seemed to think that because the boy has always received A grades in all his subjects in school that he should be more serious in his play attitudes." When I was eleven she claimed dismissively, "Sonny has very little interest in farming and that he would rather read books or play sports."

When I was thirteen, she was "anxious to discuss the matter of Sonny becoming a bit cocky in his attitudes both at home and at the Hebrew School he attends." It seems I did "not tell her of all the things that are going on in school." She complained that I was going to a junior prom (I have no memory of this) that evening and "had not even told her" the dance was to take place. "He also did not order any flowers for his date (aged 13?) and Mrs. Spiro was quite concerned about this, feeling that people may talk." My foster mother seems to have worried a good deal about others' views of me. "Foster mother showed a great deal of concern," the visitor records, "about what the neighbors would think of Sonny's behavior in regard to the fact that he is quite thoughtless about minor things." The visitor added, insightfully, "It appears that foster parents feel that Sonny is above average and they fear that people will think he is just an ordinary boy."

Helen's complaints about my shortcomings, however, took much less of her time with the visitor than "complaints in regard to money." She objected to the state's restrictions on paying her for my clothes for me, claiming when I was fourteen "that the board payments are not sufficient to even cover a substantial part of the cost of raising a boy." The visitors, in turn, seemed exasperated with Helen. "Worker had to listen to the usual complaints of a financial nature," one noted. Several months later, the same visitor maintained, "It is typical of her to bring up money and visitor had had some difficulty in steering her back into discussion of the boy and his adjustment." I am moved by the expressions of wounded professionalism from my state social worker protectors. In early high school, for example, another visitor lamented, "It appears to Mrs. Spiro that visitor's visits to the home are only to discuss finances and worker has found it very difficult to steer the conversation away from her financial problems to Isaac."

I would come home every day right after school, except for my three weeks on the baseball team. Missing the bus meant a long and tiring walk home, and even during the few years I walked from the Main Street apartment Helen expected me home soon after school. Before I could play with Gerry and before I did my homework I had to do my chores around the house. In addition to taking out the trash and shoveling snow, I was responsible for vacuuming the rugs and floors after the Spiros bought an Electrolux, and I became quite good at it. I rarely complained, even though Helen was a tough task master, certainly not as much as I did about her insistence that I wear rubbers if rain were predicted or sweaters if the sun wasn't shining. But, like any kid, I cut corners, literally and figuratively, and Helen almost always noticed. The discovery of dust under "their" bed led to long lectures about my irresponsibility, to me and then to social workers, one of whom reported, "Isaac does a lot of work around the house." She complained that I was "obstinate" or "thoughtless." I replied with arguments about justice and fairness that centered on Gerry not having to clean his house.

Not that I was missing an exciting post-school social scene. Millis had no ice cream soda culture for after school hanging out. What really curtailed my school social life, however, was Shabbos, since Friday and Saturday football and baseball games or weekend trips for movies or pizza in Milford and Framingham were where things were happening. Thank goodness for weekday activities, especially basketball and the school glee club. Helen let me go to some basketball games, especially when we lived within walking distance of the school. I was not caught up as much in basketball as in baseball and had never played, though I did throw rolled up socks into a cigar box next to my pillow from various distances in my bedroom. But I certainly talked a good game, knowing exactly how Bob Cousy, the tiny Celtic, could outplay the giant Laker George Mikan.

Much more important in providing me my school crowd was music. I couldn't read music and never had lessons, but I loved to sing so my main school activity was the glee club. I picked up my part from the piano and the people around me the first time we practiced a piece and then I just knew it. Music not only gave me friends and activities at school; it was one of the few fun things I associate with life at home, as well. When chores were done and I turned from housework to homework I listened to music on the radio as I did my lessons, usually to disc jockey Bob Clayton on Boston's WHDH. I had ferocious arguments with the cool kids like Billy Keough, who liked rhythm and blues and rock and roll, while I stuck to popular music as ballads and love songs. Bill Haley's "Rock Round the Clock" and Elvis's "Blue Suede Shoes" were not to my taste. I preferred Bob Clayton's taste: Patti Page's "Tennessee Waltz," Teresa Brewer's "How Do You Speak to an Angel," Eddie Fisher's

"Lady of Spain," plus songs of the Italian crooners, Perry Como, Al Martino, Dean Martin, and Vic Damone. I learned the words to their songs and followed the rankings on Snooky Lanson's weekly *Your Hit Parade* almost as avidly as the American League pennant race.

I had been given a small portable phonograph, a box-like record player, maybe a foot square, as a bar mitzvah present and I had a few 45s like Nat King Cole's "Too Young" and Eddie Fisher's "Oh Mein Papa," which I bought on trips to Milford, where Helen took me to get haircuts. This phonograph also introduced me to classical music. In my junior year in high school, I bought a 33 rpm record, advertised in the Boston Globe as "selections from the world's great music." It had twelve short excerpts from what I discovered years later were pieces from the romantic period, not a bad way to begin an appreciation of "great music." Phrases from "Scheherazade," "La Mer," or "L'Après-midi d'un faune" decades later still remind me of peaceful interludes in my room in Millis. Once when I was in the dentist's chair, Dr. Brown mocked my musical tastes. The Browns went to Boston's Symphony Hall on Friday nights, which we Maels knew because we kept track of the goyische habits of Millis's Jewish elite. As Dr. Brown prepared to invade my mouth, I mentioned Tchaikovsky's "Waltz of the Flowers." "Trash," he informed me. I stuck with Billy Eckstein and Johnny Ray.

Music, in fact, provided a ticket out of Millis. My sophomore year I was chosen, along with Dick Baramshian, a barrel-chested Armenian student with a beautiful bass voice, to represent Millis High School at the all-state choral festival in Springfield. Helen let me go because our bus got us there before sundown on Friday and we returned on Sunday. We stayed in private homes near the host school, so I didn't have to drive on Shabbos either. Used to singing in a glee club of twenty-five, Dick and I sang that weekend with a chorus of three hundred. Even more thrilling, for the first time, I was away from the Spiros and Maels. In the ten years since I had come to Millis I had never stayed overnight in a friend's house; in Springfield Dick Baramshian and I talked each night till 2 am. He hummed the music to help me learn my tenor part and I described the arcane principles of kosher eating, to explain why I ate so selectively.

One of those two late nights was one of the few times when some-one from a neighboring town to Millis, who didn't know me well, asked about my family and why my name was not Spiro. I was a "state kid," I explained, describing what that meant. When he probed more and asked about my real parents, I told him I knew nothing about them and that I wasn't interested in knowing. When the state brought the subject up my response was the same. Asked in high school by a visitor if I wanted to discuss my "family background," I apparently made this clear. *"The father's visits are rather unevent-ful and evidently are not too meaningful to the boy."* Helen, herself, confirmed my lack of interest in the subject. "Worker discussed with Mrs. Spiro, Isaac's feelings about his own family. She reiterated that Isaac has little feeling of connection with them as being his family. He hasn't said anything or asked about his mother. Mrs. Spiro says she can handle this if he does ask. She feels Isaac knows his mother is deceased."

In the small pond of the Millis Consolidated School I became a big fish. I shed shyness as I realized my schoolmates enjoyed being with me because I talked easily and endlessly with everyone. The girls especially liked that I was funny, but most kids liked my company and my energy. And so I usually got picked or elected to get things done. The list is familiar: assistant editor of the school paper, *The Live Wire*, in junior year, editor senior year; student council presi-dent junior year; class president senior year. My classmates respected me and my good grades but saw my leadership rooted more in my fairness and enthusiasm than in thoughtfulness or smarts. No one—including me—considered me an intellectual, or "egghead." I was a nice guy who happened to get good grades; I was organized and got things done. And, it should be noted, I was willing to share my homework. Nor, I should add, do I have any memories of anti-Sem-itism at school. It didn't come with small town rural life in New England, except on the one occasion when handyman Rufus told my foster mother and me he had been "Jewed down" by another customer, a phrase I didn't understand.

The president of the senior class had to make sure the class raised several thousand dollars to pay for the April class trip to Washington, DC. I organized "penny sales," for which we collected canned goods and clothing for auctioning to the community in the fall and winter. For pickup and delivery, I was embarrassed that Uncle Eddy, my classmate Marilyn's dad, was more dependable than either of my foster parents. We also raised money with our senior play, "We Shrunk the Family Tree," a forgettable family comedy from the 1940s written by Hildegarde Dolson, in which I, still dreaming of Broadway, played the high-school-aged son of the town banker (and wore a pink button-down shirt, charcoal gray trousers, and white buck shoes). I did the job of class president well enough to get us to Washington. What thrilled us most was not, of course, the grandeur of public Washington but the exhilarating freedom of a weeklong stay in a hotel, gossiping about rumored and real couplings, and getting to know our teacher chaperones and the bus driver.

I was busy outside of school as well, joining the Millis-Medway chapter of DeMolay my first year in high school. This organization was founded by the Masons in 1919 from a concern over the plight of teenage boys who had lost their fathers in World War I. For two years I was caught up in the hocus-pocus password world of secret handshakes and colorful medieval capes. Selected to be chapter "orator," I offered set speeches at meetings about medieval Knights Templar and heroic feats of the chivalrous crusader Jacques DeMolay. Decades later, I am professionally interested in Masonic history as any eighteenth-century scholar must be, but by junior year DeMolay's theatrics and pageantry had lost its appeal—and all of a sudden it seemed too goyische. I moved on to heavy-duty activism in the Jewish youth group, AZA.

Sponsored by the Jewish fraternal and philanthropic organization B'nai B'rith, Aleph Zade Aleph (Hebrew letters of the alphabet) and the separate BBG (B'nai B'rith Girls) were secular clubs for Jewish teenagers first established in 1924 in Omaha, Nebraska, and by 1950 they were found across America. After attending several meetings with a friend in Framingham, I decided that Millis and Medway should have its own chapter and with Gerry's help pulled it off. Since chapters named themselves, we chose for ours "Alexander D. Goode," the name of the Jewish chaplain who with his Protestant and Catholic colleagues went down with the USS *Dorchester* in

February 1943. Hit directly by a U-boat torpedo, the ship sank in the icy waters off Greenland, killing all but 230 of its 900 American servicemen headed to combat in Europe. Survivors said the chaplains gave their life jackets to soldiers and then with linked arms prayed as the ship sank. This choice of a patriotic American role model over Jewish seekers of social justice was reflective of my high school Republicanism.

My social life the last two years of school was AZA. Because there was great interest in chapter cooperation for Jewish activism and dances, AZA had plenty of weekend regional conferences, and since I was the Aleph Godol, the chapter president (literally, the big A), I went twice, to Lynn and to Dorchester. To a country bumpkin these cities were dazzling. I felt like I was back with my city cousins in my foster mother's cousins' club, and I decided that urban Jews were neat. After heady sessions on how to raise money for Israel, America's new democratic ally in the Middle East, we had dances, usually with bands, for how else were young American Jewish boys going to meet young American Jewish girls? This was a new and rather daunting world for me. I had no problem asserting myself about how to help Israel, but didn't know how to put myself forward at dances, so I spent most of them chatting with other shy AZA guys and sipping a cream soda.

I did know how to dance. As part of her strategy to mature and polish me, my foster mother signed me up for weekly dancing lessons with Miss Santoro, who devoted herself through most of the 1940s and 1950s to the nearly impossible task of bringing a modicum of glamour and sophistication to Millis. Her lessons took the form of mini cotillions at the Grange Hall, a beautiful white-columned wooden building in Millis Center. Most farming communities had these impressive halls, built after the Civil War by the Grange, the fraternal organization that brought farmers together for political and social life. Miss Santoro enrolled only couples, so I went with cousin Marilyn or cousin Barbie. Hair slathered with Vitalis, reeking of Old Spice, and uncomfortable in a tie and jacket, I walked arm in arm with my cousin across the Grange floor to the record player's musical beat, bowed before Miss Santoro, and said, "May I present

my partner Marilyn Mael." Then came waltz or samba lessons, followed an hour later by the same ritual retreat, the presentation, the
bow, the arm and arm.

I didn't really date in high school, despite Miss Santoro's lessons
and the AZA dances. While I "went out" a lot by the time I was fifteen, it was always as part of a group, either at school occasions or
at AZA affairs. I talked easily with girls, but never about feelings
or emotions. In the summer, when I hung out at the Jewish hotels,
I never sought out a girlfriend. We'd watch movies at Cohen's in
a group, and at Novicks's rec hall, beside their new pool, we had
frappes or danced to the juke box, but never with special partners.
I tangoed to "I Love Paris" with whoever was there. Nor did I feel
bad about not having a girlfriend. I was busy enough forming my
own self and was perhaps too preoccupied with schoolwork to think
I needed someone else to be complete.

The self I was forging was not that of a sensitive, introspective
young man escaping provincial banality and stifling home life by
reading Dickens or Dos Passos. I read nothing more serious than *The
Hardy Boys* and all the Penny Parker and Nancy Drew books. I liked
life in Millis and the respect of friends and teachers that my conventional role as engaged school leader produced. I had no models of
thoughtful, reflective people, either in my family or in my imagination, and no teacher introduced me to a wider world of culture and
ideas. Like the Maels, my teachers were decent people who cared
about me and shared, as I did, the Eisenhower era's suspicion of intellect. The elementary school teachers who followed the wicked Miss
Hartigan—Mrs. Horan, Mrs. Enegren, Mrs. Brennan, Mrs. Fernald,
and Mrs. Blum—were middle-aged married women who lived in
Millis. They knew about my parentage and were supportive. They
merge in a memory of maternal reassurance and concern with only
Mrs. Blum standing out as a teacher with zest and character, insisting, for example, that her sixth graders witness the signing of the
NATO treaty on the TV she brought to school for that purpose. As
if this were not radical enough, Mrs. Blum also urged us to tell our
parents to support Harold Stassen, the former liberal Republican
governor from Minnesota, who ran for president every four years
for decades.

Nor were my handful of high school teachers particularly imaginative either. I knew them well since the same teachers taught the varying levels of the four-year curriculum and, just as important, because they were locals. Mrs. Gavin, who taught all the science, and Mrs. Kenny, who taught all the math, were sisters who lived in Millis, and Mr. Doyle, who taught history and civics, lived in Medway. The language and English teachers tended to be younger out-of-towners, who didn't last long at our school. They were nice, helpful people, and with my good grades and "school spirit" I was usually their pet. But they were not intellectually stimulating, though such thoughts never occurred to me then.

High school students could choose the "college" course or the "commercial" course in high school, with about ten from my class in each. Everyone took the same English and history classes, but while I did algebra and French, the commercial kids did typing and bookkeeping. Where we really felt the school's small size was in its limited offerings. Only one year of Latin and two of French were taught. We learned enough French, however, so that when I had my appendix out in sophomore year my classmates wrote to me in the hospital with the same question: "Ou avez-vous mal?" Mrs. Kenny taught math through trigonometry, but not calculus; her sister taught no more science than first-year chemistry and first-year physics. In English we read canonical texts like *Silas Marner* and *Julius Caesar*, but I never wrote an essay or paper until my senior year, when I chose Theodore Dreiser's *An American Tragedy* from a list of books to read and write about. To say I wrote a report exaggerates my achievement, however, since I copied most of it from an encyclopedia entry and two books on Dreiser. I assumed, correctly, I could get away with what I now recognize as plagiarism—and even then sensed was wrong—since I used the library in neighboring Medfield. Such was the beginning of my career in scholarly research.

I did well in all my courses, science, social studies, languages, math and English, because I diligently did my homework, even as I listened to Patti Page and Nat King Cole, and because I studied before tests, unlike most of my classmates. Getting good grades became an important part of my sense of self, of my identity, not, heaven forbid, as an intellectual, but as someone who was smart. Doing well at school was one of the few things I did other than going to shul that pleased my foster mother while impressing my social workers, and since I never became a star pitcher, good grades gave me prominence in school, as well. Imagine then how upset I was when Mr. Brown, my champion during the school bus war, announced in the winter of senior year that our class of twenty was to have two valedictorians, because Shirley Spencer and I had exactly the same grade point average. A nice enough, quiet girl, uninvolved with school activities, Shirley was in the commercial course, and I had never considered her a rival for the honor. But exemplar of school spirit that I was, I gamely accepted Mr. Brown's decision to designate as valedictorians 10 percent of the class, nor did I gloat (outwardly) when most of the prizes at graduation went to me, since previous elitist benefactors, it turned out, had seen fit to honor distinction in history, math, and science and not in typing and bookkeeping.

My graduation speech in 1955 was a Cold War indictment of communism, a call for complacent America to root out communism at home and roll it back abroad. I described communism as a pernicious threat to religious values, mine and America's, while warning of its seductive appeal to idealists and well-intentioned do-gooders. Though much of the speech was lifted from J. Edgar Hoover's *Masters of Deceit*, it was sincere and heartfelt, for to the extent that the self I forged in high school had any intellectual context it was a fascination with politics and political ideas. My interest was longstanding and noticeable. When I was eleven, my foster mother complained that I disrespectfully "butted into" family conversations with "definite ideas of my own on politics and about who should win elections." The social workers noticed this, too, one writing two years later: "The boy has always had a very strong interest in politics and national elections."

I was a fierce follower of Wisconsin senator Joseph McCarthy, whose name came to describe the years in the early 1950s when America was caught up in an anti-communist witch hunt—not my reading of it then, of course. I was excited when, a year before my bar mitzvah, in February 1950, McCarthy, speaking in Wheeling, West Virginia, claimed to have in his hand "a list of 205 communists in

Fig. 10 | Isaac with Christian Herter, governor of Massachusetts, at the American Legion–sponsored Boys State summer immersion program on the workings of government, 1954

the State Department." He and his Senate Committee investigated and "exposed" alleged communists in the government, the university, and even the army.

I had no problems with the bullying tactics of McCarthy's committee and was proud that the committee's bullying chief of staff, always at McCarthy's side, was the Jewish Roy Cohn. He provided for me a powerful rejoinder to what I saw as the mistaken and malicious linkage of communism with disloyal Jews, which emerged from the coverage of the Rosenberg espionage trial. Fascinated with Cohn, I raced home to see the Army-McCarthy hearings on TV in 1954. Those hearings and the Senate's censure of McCarthy would break McCarthy's spell over over America, but Cohn remained a political hero for me. Decades later I saw him in an airport, much flabbier, but still with his unmistakable sunken eyes; some years after that I, like many others, saw a very different Roy Cohn recreated on Broadway in Tony Kushner's phenomenally successful play "Angels in America."

Like all the Maels, my politics were deeply conservative, yet colored by populist and egalitarian instincts. Democrats were evil because they were soft on godless, atheistic communism, but also because they were the party of corrupt urban union bosses, elitist intellectuals, and aristocratic Roosevelts and Harrimans. Not only were we Maels Republicans, but in the postwar struggle for the soul of the party we were solidly in the ultraconservative camp of Senator Robert Taft, from Ohio, as he opposed, unsuccessfully, the more establishment, liberal Republican wing of bankers and businessmen, represented by New York's governor Thomas Dewey and then by Dwight Eisenhower. We applauded Taft's more successful effort to curb the power of unions, as embodied in the anti-labor legislation that carried his name, the Taft-Hartley Act, restricting the right to strike.

In those complacent Cold War years, growing up conservative in rural Massachusetts was easy enough, however counterintuitive it may seem in light of widely chronicled stories of the urban Jewish-American experience. It was helped by the fact that Millis was at or near the center of the state and national Republican politics. The Republican governor of Massachusetts, Christian Herter, had an estate in the gentry fringe on the northeast edge of town. The elegant, soft-spoken, patrician-looking son of an artist, who had grown up in Europe, had acquired the Millis home to add to his others. While seldom spotted in town when he was governor from 1953 to 1957, this home was his legal residence, and he was always referred to, we proudly noted, as "Christian Herter from Millis," as he would be when he served as Eisenhower's secretary of state in the late 1950s.

The Republican senator from Massachusetts, Leverett Saltonstall, lived in the next town, Dover, the Brahmin enclave that needed no public school. In his Senate years from 1944 to 1967, "Lev," the tall, thin, gaunt, and quintessential laconic card-carrying Yankee, was the face of Massachusetts Republicanism, and the face would on very rare occasions be seen in Millis. If this were not enough hometown Republican pride, there was also our US congressman, who for all the years I lived in Millis was the Republican Joe Martin, who was from the next town, Norfolk. He sat in Congress from 1925 to 1967, serving as the Speaker of the House of Representatives from 1947 to 1949 and then again in my junior and senior years, from 1953 to 1955. Martin was not, like Herter and Saltonstall, from the graceful, if slightly awkward, Harvard educated elite; he was Mr. Ordinary Guy, a plain-looking, somewhat short and disheveled, blunt, and straight-talking critic of FDR's New Deal, embodying Main Street, small town values, my values. I even have memories of Joe Martin showing up at Millis Memorial Day ceremonies.

My conservative politics, nourished by these Republican local luminaries, found explicit and dramatic expression in my junior year, when I was chosen by the teachers to represent Millis High School at Massachusetts Boys State, sponsored by the American Legion and held in June each year at the University of Massachusetts campus in Amherst. Founded in 1935 as a national weeklong civics lesson for high school leaders in the workings of their state government, with students running for state offices and role playing as legislators, Boys State had also become in the mid-1950s a week of anti-communist indoctrination with lectures from the Legion officials and films that showed the map of the world's countries overspread with red paint. No surprise, then, that I loved Boys State. When I ran for Massachusetts lieutenant governor in the mock elections, my campaign speech was a thundering attack on communism, which began, I thought rather dramatically, by quoting Marx's *Communist Manifesto*, that "a spectre is haunting Europe— the spectre of Communism," which I later adapted for my graduation valedictory. I lost the election, but my speech was so stirring that the American Legion decided to use it for school programs they sponsored around the State. In what became my first lesson in the power of words, I was then selected as an alternate to Boys Nation and invited to return as a counselor at the next year's Boys State. The two boys elected governor and lieutenant governor did not get sick, alas, so I never went to Boys Nation, where I would have met President Eisenhower, as young Bill Clinton several years later would meet John F. Kennedy. But the Legion did bring me to Boston to meet Governor Herter, who seemed pleased that I was from Millis when the Legion State Commander presented him with a copy of my anti-communist manifesto.

America was, of course, actually fighting communism on real battlefields in these years. Harry Truman proved that conservative claims that Democrats were soft on communism were wrong by involving America in a bloody, hot war against it. The Korean war from June 1950 to July 1953 saw US troops fighting alongside the army of the Republic of Korea against the forces of the People's Republic of Korea, supported by, as we called it then, Red China and the Soviet Union. I learned on one of my father Max's visits that my brother Sigmund was in the war, and I pushed it out of mind. I would only learn some years later that he had been drafted shortly after he and Helen were married, and he served in Korea for two years as a radio operator at the front lines. When he returned to Peabody and had difficulty finding work, she apparently suggested he use his GI Bill benefits and return to Boston University. Building on his war experience and the discovery he could write easily and well, Sigmund majored in communications and embarked on a career in journalism. I know nothing of Leon's story in my high school years; Max never mentioned him, and I have never been able to find records about his years in the Danvers Asylum.

My interest in politics gradually shaped who I wanted to be and what I wanted to do "when I grew up." The short-lived fantasy of singing on Broadway was replaced for several years by a resolve to be a rabbi or a cantor, enthusiastically encouraged by my foster mother. I never envisioned myself pouring over talmudic texts or providing pastoral wisdom, only leading services with Zayde's dramatic flair. This wish, too, faded, not because of a spiritual crisis but from an emerging sense that I wanted a career in politics or government. In my senior yearbook I put as my goal in life "to be the secretary of state."

It wouldn't be easy, and being a "state kid" and Jewish wouldn't help. But I was convinced that someday, if I worked hard enough, I just might run American foreign policy and stop communism. Effort and enterprise made anything possible, I assumed, for in constructing self and defining my personality and character in high school. I believed in my Americanism rhetoric equating industriousness and hard work with moral virtue. The Maels and my foster father worked hard, and while they were by no means well-to-do, they were not poor, not even Saul. Their lives were work and prayer, without, it seemed to me, vacations, hobbies, or leisure activities.

By my early teens, I saw no value in inactivity. Summers were no longer for carefree play but a time to work and earn money. When we moved to the nice house on Pleasant Street, I picked blackberries from the huge patch in the field below the house and sold them by the quart to the Jewish hotels. While I was in high school I worked every summer. One summer I worked on a nearby farm clearing rocks from a large field of vegetables and painting fences. Another summer I polished screws and bolts at a machine shop on Main Street owned by the father of a classmate. Best of all was the summer I worked for the Registry of Motor Vehicles in Boston, next to North Station and Boston Garden. The commissioner of motor vehicles, Rudy King, was another important Republican from Millis, a former Speaker of the Massachusetts House of Representatives, who found jobs every summer for a few local kids. The work, filing paper copies of traffic violations, was tedious, but I was introduced to a wonderful new world of coffee breaks, lunch hours, and overtime. The summer workers were a diverse lot, all political appointments and exotic to provincial me. I met a Black person for the first time, the son of a State House policeman from Stoughton. He became my lunchtime buddy and tutor in the fine art of looking at women in their summer dresses without appearing to do so. He also schooled me in how to maximize overtime, so by August I was earning $55.00 a week, about as much as Saul, and saving most of it. My bank account, begun after my bar mitzvah, grew each summer. I vowed not to touch it until college, the first step on the road to the office of secretary of state.

That a "state kid" would go to college was highly unusual. Most left school at sixteen, got jobs, and with financial independence, passed out of the foster care system. Nor was college part of Mael family practice. My cousins tended to begin work in the cow business after high school. I proved the exception, but not because any one in my family or a proverbial beloved teacher nurtured my mind, pushed me, and had faith I would make it. What I had instead was the Commonwealth of Massachusetts, which played that role and played it well. In my corner were numerous social workers who moved from early relieved observations that I was "normal and bright" to delight that I did well in school, observing when I was ten that I was "undoubtedly college material." Soon the social worker was telling me and my foster mother that I "needed to set a goal in life" and "think of college." If I applied myself and continued to do well in school he would recommend to his director that the state provide some financial assistance for college. And he did. "Worker would recommend very highly that this Department assist this boy in pursuing his college education since he is an extremely bright individual and has excellent potentials for college training."

As my social workers reinforced this message, I eagerly internalized it. I would have beamed, I'm sure, had I known that one social worker countered Helen's objections to my joining the baseball team sophomore year with the advice that "scholarship committees always consider extra-curricular activities on the part of a student applying." When I was a junior, the social worker walked me and Helen through the complicated process of college admissions, using that year's application to the University of Massachusetts as a guide. In the fall he helped me fill out my various applications. More helpful still, it was my social worker, not a teacher or guidance counselor, who knew about the alternative Sunday sitting for the College Board Exam at Simmons College in Boston, scheduled for Orthodox Jews who could not write on Saturday.

For these reasons my attitude to the social workers changed as I moved through high school. I had disliked their visits, though never as much as Max's, because they brought to the surface what I suppressed, the ambiguities of my life in Millis. By senior year I looked forward to seeing them every two months or so. When they came, I still had to acknowledge being a ward of the state, but in exchange I got to hear them tell me how different I was from most kids in foster care, how special and important I was. These were messages I did not often hear from Helen and Saul.

The officers of the state were particularly concerned that Helen understand the cost of college and hoped the Spiros would contribute some part, however small. They promised to bear the extra expense of board and room in college until I was twenty-one, much longer than usual. The assumption that the Spiros would help was not unreasonable, since the social workers commented frequently about how close this foster arrangement was and about the equally unusual "very, very, lovely and spacious eight room house with plenty of backyard for the boy to play baseball" in which we lived. Helen, in turn, thought the state should provide more than the room and board it usually gave her. The exasperated social worker noted, "The foster mother was not completely satisfied with the extent of the aid this Department might give. This is not unusual since there is always some bickering over finances with this particular fo. mo."

Helen thought they would help. She had been putting some of her board checks aside in a special savings account, she told the social worker, and hoped to use that money to assist me at college. But if Saul's work continued as bad as it had been, she couldn't promise not to use some of that savings now. The state social worker was not surprised: "There is no doubt they will plead poverty." Apparently, few, if any, foster mothers were as successful with their charges as Helen was, but they knew her also as uniquely tough about money. Another social worker explained why help was unlikely in terms that glossed the truth with language tapping into anti-Semitic stereotypes: "The foster mother is a difficult person to work with in view of the fact that she is continually complaining about inadequate allowances and trying to chisel a few dollars here or there."

I forgive the anonymous social worker this minor transgression, given how helpful this person and her/his colleagues were in shaping my life. Today, hearing or reading about foster care often involves a gruesome tale of neglect or abuse. My story is different, from a different time in America, to be sure. My development through childhood and adolescence testifies to the involvement and dedication of countless conscientious, committed, and compassionate public servants working for the Massachusetts Division of Child Guardianship. I like to think that in its way the state was the supportive substitute father that Saul was not, alongside Helen, my stalwart foster mother, advocates and nurturers both.

In any event, in 1954, the state encouraged Helen and me to apply for college scholarships. The state thought I was a natural for a possibility unearthed by Mr. Brown, the annual award of the Millis chapter of the American Legion of $250. Helen, however, was reluctant to apply for this scholarship because "she does not want to give the people in the town the impression that they are needy." Helen insisted that "with our social standing in the community we would not wish to plead poverty." Stymied here, the ever-resource-ful state enlisted my foster mother's cooperation in an effort to get Max to help. In the spring of my junior year she persuaded me to ask Max to save $5 a week for my college costs. Since this initiative was accompanied by the state's suggestion that Max be invited to my high school graduation, an idea I opposed as strongly as Helen, I refused to ask him for the assistance. Thwarted here, as well, the social worker ruefully quoted Helen's honest response: "It wouldn't be good for him to attend graduation since it would be difficult to explain his presence to friends." And the visitor added a recurring observation: "He [Isaac] never discusses his family with anyone and whenever I hint at a discussion about his family he always avoids the subject."

Helen then identified another possible benefactor. The father of the allergy specialist she took me to in Boston summered in one of Millis's Jewish hotels. Apparently, he was impressed with me because I attended Shabbos services at shul so regularly. Helen told a skep-tical social worker that this man had promised to help finance my education if I agreed to become a rabbi. Since I had pushed aside any thought of being a rabbi long before my senior year, I never knew whether the offer was real or a scheme hatched by Helen, who was dubious about my ambition to study politics and the law and to become secretary of state. I knew that, and the social work-ers did, too; one of them wrote, "She felt that he should not pick some kind of a profession like being a lawyer or a doctor and felt that he should do something more practical." Surprising perhaps for a "Jewish mother," but consistent with a rabbinic career.

My ambitions raised the larger question of what colleges I was thinking about, which further complicated the issue of who was paying, since the costs of the schools I applied to varied dramati-cally. The state urged me to apply to the University of Massachusetts. The state's room and board payments would suffice there, and the very low tuition could be met by a combination of a scholarship and a job. My foster mother urged Brandeis University in nearby

Waltham. Founded just seven years prior in 1948, Brandeis—named after the first Jewish Supreme Court justice, Louis Dembitz Brandeis, from (of all places) Louisville, Kentucky, by way of Harvard Law School—was already beloved among Jews as America's first "Jewish university," with kosher food to prove it. Brandeis, Helen declared, was a small college where Isaac "could better express himself" and "where he would be within his element." In my hubris, I wanted to apply to Harvard, the breeding ground of secretaries of state, if not always a welcoming home for those in my element.

That I even thought of Harvard was the product of a friendship I developed in high school with a do-gooder in Millis's small gentry community. Through her, like Gatsby, I saw the light of a distant other. Wedding philanthropic to elitist instincts, Polly Baker was the principal force in Millis trying to raise consciousness about and money for the new educational television station, WGBH in Boston. When she approached the principal for a student to help her spread the gospel, Mr. Brown suggested me, and thus began my introduction to New England's WASP aristocracy. An energetic Yankee in her early forties, pleasant and easy to talk to, Mrs. Baker dressed in simple, practical clothes. We worked together for months on the campaign for channel 4 and, as we talked about my plans for college, she advised me to think of Harvard, brushing aside my concerns for cost and class with descriptions of scholarship possibilities that were news to me. Her relative was headmaster of Milton Academy, a prestigious prep school in Milton, Massachusetts, where her boys were at school, she told me, and through him she knew all about how to get into the Ivy League.

Mrs. Baker invited me to her house one Sunday morning to learn more about Harvard from her son Toby, who had brought home some of his classmates from Milton for the weekend. She picked me up in her Ford station wagon (with its signature wooden sides) and drove me to her estate on the Dover side of town. I soon found myself playing touch football on a huge leaf-covered lawn with three "preppies," the first I'd ever seen. Toby and his friends were slightly younger than I and wore button-down blue shirts, chinos, and penny loafers with no socks. They were too well bred to comment on my plaid shirt, dress pants, dark socks, and dress shoes.

There was lots of talk after the game about the superiority of BBC commercial-free television and the superiority of Harvard. Apply by all means, the boys urged: "Polly says you have a chance." After that memorable morning, which I remembered every time I saw news footage of the Kennedys playing touch football at Hyannis, I submitted an application, despite grave doubts about fitting in, let alone getting in.

I applied to the University of Massachusetts and Brandeis as well, and through the entire process Henry Doyle—civics teacher, assistant principal, and the school's only guidance counselor —took charge, shepherding me through it all. A tall, thin, wiry man with a pocked face, Mr. Doyle was "Hand Grenade Hank" to his students because he spent so much time regaling us with his exploits in World War II. As if he were on a military mission, Mr. Doyle spent hours talking with me about each school and drove me to all three interviews. I found the University of Massachusetts Amherst, with its high-rise buildings, too vast and cold. Moreover, I thought I could do better than UMass, where college-bound seniors from Millis traditionally went. That I was told during my interview that I was accepted only confirmed my misgivings.

At Brandeis I was interviewed in what seemed to be a medieval castle, an inheritance, I learned, from the Middlesex Medical School, the previous occupant of the grounds. I was further confused about the place when I met Charles Ruggles, the dean of this first Jewish college. Thinner than everyone in my shul and certainly more elegant, Dean Ruggles wore a fitted suit and a bow tie, the first I'd ever seen. I wondered if he, too, was inherited along with the medical school's castle.

Hand Grenade Hank also braved Boston and Cambridge traffic and found Harvard's Admissions office, then in a small colonial house on a hard-to-locate Cambridge side street. It proved to be all either of us saw of the university, since we had to dash home before rush hour. When I was ushered in to meet the director of admissions, Mr. Doyle stayed in the outer office, nervously flipping through issues of the *New Yorker*, a magazine neither of us had ever seen before. Mr. Wallace McDonald, a handsome man in a warm tweed jacket, blue button-down shirt, chinos, penny loafers (with

Fig. 11 |
Isaac Kramnick,
high school
graduation, Millis,
MA, 1955

socks), and a striped repp tie, was wonderfully gracious to me, and in our conversation, it seemed to me, he took inordinate interest in my foster-care status. He then asked me what good book I'd recently read, the open-ended question intended, I realized years later, to pave the way for subtler questions about plot development, or character analysis, or wherever the canonical book might take a sophisticated college interviewer. When I answered *The Lou Gehrig Story*, the outwardly unflappable Mr. McDonald moved to another topic.

When asked by the state, Mr. Doyle agreed to engineer my nomination for the American Legion scholarship over Helen's opposition. Years later I learned from the file that he and my social worker had met during my junior year to plan a strategy for getting me into college. When Brandeis accepted me and offered a tuition scholarship, Mr. Doyle cautioned me to wait until I heard from Harvard, even though Helen had already sent a $50 deposit from my savings account.

My other teachers urged Brandeis, telling me that if I went to Harvard I'd "become an atheist and a communist," but Mr. Doyle, no less Catholic and anti-communist than they, wanted me to wait. He was motivated, perhaps, by pride in his high school, which had not sent a graduate to Harvard in anyone's memory, and partly from his realization as a civics teacher that "making it against the odds Horatio Alger stories" were sweeter and more meaningful at Harvard than at Brandeis, even in the McCarthy era. He also knew from our long car rides that Harvard was my preference as well. No surprise, then, that Mr. Doyle was the first person I called after Harvard's thick envelope arrived. I told him that my acceptance came with an $850 scholarship to pay its $800 tuition. Hand Grenade Hank had out-hustled and outfoxed Helen; Harvard it would be.

Harvard had accepted me as one of that year's ten "wild cards," I learned years later at a university dinner when I, then a Harvard instructor, happened to sit next to Wallace McDonald, by then dean of freshmen. The admissions committee, he confided, had the authority to fill 1 percent of the class with otherwise qualified and interesting applicants who fell short of the customary thresholds, in my case weak SAT scores and a less-than-challenging high school curriculum. From my case file I would learn that the Division of Child Guardianship had a hand in this, too, having provided letters to one Eric Cutler, assistant to the Harvard College Committee on Admissions, reviewing my history from Worcester State Hospital to Boys State. Harvard, in turn, was concerned about how much financial help its wild card might get from the state, a question that triggered the final round of haggling over money between the state and Helen, this time with me present and participating for the first time.

Helen, Mr. Lenk (the first social worker whose name I remember), and I had a financial summit meeting a week after my high school graduation. Mr. Lenk put pieces of paper on the kitchen table with calculations showing that room, board, books, and spending money plus tuition for my first year totaled just over $2,100. All but $400 would be covered by Harvard's scholarship; the American Legion award, which I had won; money from the state; and part of my anticipated earnings from my summer job, again at the Registry of Motor Vehicles in Boston. He asked my foster mother how much money the Spiros could provide. Helen's response captured the complex and contradictory person she was. She was "proud of Sonny," she told Mr. Lenk, who looked so out of place in his seersucker suit in our kitchen, "unbelievably proud of him and of what he has accomplished." She was proud, too, she added, of what she had done for me, for she "had to fight the state at every turn." But, unfortunately, she couldn't help financially. The money saved to help me in college was gone: "Foster mother reported that this money has been spent to buy the house and she does not have this money now. Foster mother also stated that she felt that it was her money and she should be entitled to use it as she saw fit. She almost cried as she said she had planned to help Isaac financially but her husband's business is poor and she can't."

When Mr. Lenk let slip that he expected as much, she shifted from tearful regret to snappy combat, complaining that Mr. Lenk should not have discussed with me how much of the state's payments would go with me to Harvard. She had assumed, quite correctly, that I had no idea that the state was paying her anything for my care. While I knew nothing about money ostensibly set aside from board payments, I was deeply hurt and saddened to hear that there would be no financial help from what I considered my family.

I said virtually nothing for most of the budget summit, though I was fascinated by this first glimpse into the finances of my foster care, which even included protracted negotiations over whether Helen or the state would pay for the sheets and blankets for my dorm room. I spoke twice. I endorsed Mr. Lenk's suggestion that the state's forthcoming summer board money go to me and not my foster mother, an idea she flatly rejected: "Mrs. Spiro stated that she would probably need to use the board received during the summer months and felt that this money could not be put aside for Isaac." And I agreed that since Harvard did not want me to draw down my savings, half of the remaining $400 should come from the state and half from a job I'd get on campus, which Helen thought a good idea.

I pushed aside the unpleasantness of these transactions, just as I pushed aside so much else in my early years, refusing even to enter the bargaining over the purchase of the "required" tweed jacket. I was cocky, as Helen so often chided, and confident, ready to move on, and oblivious to what was about to hit me as I left the cozy embrace of the Mael shul and tiny Millis High for Harvard Yard and the ghosts of Cotton Mather, Ralph Waldo Emerson, and Henry Adams.

CHAPTER 7

Harvard

There was a time when Harvard asked each year's incoming students to read *The Education of Henry Adams* in the summer before they arrived on campus. That tradition-laden practice had ended by my arrival in 1955, and I hope it had something to do with Adams's anti-Semitism. Instead, taking very seriously its responsibility *in loco parentis*, Harvard's dean of freshmen, the wonderfully named F. Skiddy von Stade Jr., wrote a letter to the parents of incoming freshmen asking them to describe their son and share any concerns they had about his transition to college life. Helen discussed her response with the social worker: "She wrote about how she didn't want Sonny to strain himself physically or emotionally in school as she knows sometimes adjustment in college the first year is difficult. She mentioned Isaac's adherence to Orthodox religious customs and wondered if this might come into conflict with regulations of Harvard University."

For me, freshman year at Harvard was hell, not a strain. From the moment I arrived at Grays Hall, my dorm on the Mass Avenue side of the Yard, I felt inadequate and afraid. To get to my room on the top floor I had to navigate Harvard's class structure, walking past the rooms of the rich preppies on the ground floor, then by the ordinary paying students in the middle floors, to the scholarship students' rooms in the attic-like fifth floor. The room itself was not particularly humble. It was a suite, with two small bedrooms, two beds in each, a common living room, and a bathroom. But the climb, the long climb, stamped indelibly who you were and reminded you how much further you had to go.

My three roommates, each in his own way, put an exclamation point on my overwhelming sense that I was out of place. Bill Kates, a strapping tall boy with already receding hair, played the oboe, an instrument I'd never heard of, which baffled me all the more since it hung in his mouth on the end of a tiny stick. The son of a professor at the University of Oklahoma, Bill never finished a sentence without referring to someone named Camus and something called existentialism. Lee Gold, a savvy New Yorker, was, unlike me, neither bewildered nor confused by this new environment. Brash, tough, and competitive, he immediately mastered course selection and scheduling and informed me that Harvard was going to be a piece of cake. Jay Lander, whom I knew vaguely from the Framingham chapter of AZA and whom I had requested as a roommate, was neither intimidating nor frightening, but he, too, I discovered, could hold his own in bull sessions when someone brought up names like Salinger or Nietzsche. With a social smoothness I envied, Jay seemed able to make new friends with ease.

For weeks I thought only of my inadequate preparation for Harvard, recognizing for the first time the limitations of Millis High and the provincialism of growing up with the Spiros and the Maels, which I must have shared with my social worker, Mr. Warschauer, when he visited me in my dorm six weeks into my first semester.

Isaac is constantly worrying. It turns out that he feels inferior to many of the other students in his class. He states that they seemed to have a better background and preparation for Harvard than he has. He feels that the families they come from and their schools offered these other students much more in the way of preparation for courses he is now taking. Isaac stated it has been quite a change for him to come from a small high school to Harvard University.

Like so many visitors before him, Mr. Warschauer wondered whether I was emotionally affected by my unusual life history.

During the discussion with Isaac concerning his feeling of inferiority as compared with other students worker asked if perhaps this had something to do with his family background. Isaac said this did not interfere with his adjustment at school. It seemed from his description that he reflected a feeling on his past about the Spiro foster home and the feeling he possibly has of the comparison between his home and the homes of other students in terms of familiarity with books.

Soon after arriving, first-year students wrote an essay to place us in either an honors or a regular freshman composition section. In response to our assigned topic, the decline of the theme of nature in contemporary literature, Bill Kates speculated that it followed inevitably from the urbanization of modern life and the decline of a pastoral ethos. Barely aware of what he was talking about, I squelched the urge to leave Cambridge and accepted my regular section assignment. I never told Bill, who got the honors class, about the gibberish I had written. And so began my turn inward, my response to my sense of inferiority, and the terror I felt. The affable, self-confident high school easy talker on any and all subjects stopped talking about course work with roommates, avoided late-night bull sessions when they turned to serious topics, like the existence of God, and didn't participate in classroom discussions, fearing I would be laughed at for what I said.

My sense of inferiority was not helped by the related feeling that I was out of place, different. My roommates talked incessantly about and to their parents. I didn't. I dressed differently as well, having arrived unaware of the Harvard "uniform," the tweed jacket, button-down dress shirt, tie, and chinos. Assuming the tweed was for special occasions, I wore my one other jacket, the product of protracted negotiations with the state. Most of the time I wore a plaid shirt (with a tie, to be sure) and one of the pair of trousers I had, only one of which was chinos, thus earning the label "country bumpkin" from Lee Gold. Beyond my sense of small-town provincialism was the fact that while all my roommates were Jewish, which we assumed was not coincidental, I was the only observant one, not eating *treyf* (shellfish, pork, or any meat, for that matter) my first semester. Instead, I signed up for four kosher dinners a week at Hillel House, then a long walk from Harvard Yard on Irving Street.

It seemed to me that of the four of us I alone was bothered by the pervasive WASPiness of Harvard, from its freshman dean to its dorms named Thayer, Weld, and Wigglesworth, and classroom buildings named Emerson and Lowell. When I walked by the preppies on the first floor three or four times a day, I marveled at their serenity and self-assurance, their casual manner. In my discussion sections the preppies spoke more than anyone else, usually making good sense. There were two Cabots in my class, and I was fascinated by them. I began to realize that Yankee spotting was a love-hate thing, begun probably in my friendship with Polly Baker. It had a powerful significance for my sense that I was different. More than simply a recognition of the Jewishness at my core, my fascination with Harvard's elites drew sustenance from something missing, not wealth or class but roots, history, and the continuity of family. Cabot fathers and grandfathers had from time out of mind gone to a Harvard that was, in the words of the alma mater, a fixed rock "through change and through storm."

I suspect I was not the first Jew at Harvard to come down with a case of "WASP envy." I would years later learn the sorry Harvard Jewish story. In 1900 Jews made up only 7 percent of Harvard's student body, which changed dramatically in 1905 when the college started using the College Entrance Examination Board tests as the main criterion for admission. By 1922, when the numbers of Jews had tripled to 21 percent, A. Lawrence Lowell, Harvard's president, proposed a 15 percent quota on Jews. Too many Jews could destroy Harvard, he wrote: "The summer hotel that is ruined by admitting Jews meets its fate . . . because they drive away the Gentiles, and then after the Gentiles have left, they leave also." Lowell argued that the quota was good for Jewish students, because it would dampen anti-Semitism on campus. "The anti-Semitic feeling among the students is increasing, and it grows in proportion to the increase in the number of Jews. If their number should become 40% of the student body, the race feeling would become intense."

When the proposed quota evoked much public criticism, especially in Boston newspapers, Lowell set up a committee to study Harvard's "Jewish problem." The solution was to change the notion of merit for admission from test scores to markers of personal character. Letters of recommendation became obligatory, as did photographs of applicants. Geographical diversity in the student body came to trump scholastic excellence. It worked; by the end of Lowell's presidency in 1933 the percentage of Jews at Harvard was about 15 percent, where it remained for decades.

I, of course, knew none of this in my first few weeks at Harvard, but I must have sensed its echo in the buildings and the students. Harvard seemed to me in my naïveté not unlike it did to A. Lawrence Lowell: two communities, one with competitive and ambitious Jewish city kids, and the other an even larger collection of preppies, whose historical rootedness, easy grace, and articulateness I, alas, intensely envied.

After my first terrifying weeks in the Yard I changed. My introspection made me consciously think of my own history, or lack thereof, for the first time, and the gregarious Millis teenager became a loner. When I didn't eat at Hillel, I went to meals at the cavernous Freshman Union with my roommates and laughed with them at Teddy Roosevelt's moose heads on the wall. I went to classes with them and other casual friends. But for rest of the day, unlike my roommates, who studied in Lamont, the undergraduate library next door to the Union, I studied in my room. For four years I did not study in the library. The sight of so many other students made me anxious, emphasizing dramatically the competitiveness of Harvard, in which I felt so inadequate. In my room, alone at my desk, where I spent every afternoon and evening, I had the calming illusion that only I was working, with no one around to expose me as a fraud who didn't deserve to be at Harvard.

I rarely did anything socially with my freshman roommates except go to meals. The only time outside of class I wasn't alone studying was spent with the freshman glee club, my one extracurricular activity. Still fearful of being revealed an impostor, who in this case couldn't read music, I joined the club only after I learned that everyone was accepted. Much to my amazement, most glee club members were preppies, who came from schools with numerous a cappella singing groups. They knew (and I later discovered) that our practices traditionally culminated in a joint concert with the chorus from the Windsor School, a tony private school for girls in Boston. The glee club, a diversion from studying and grist for my love-hate relations with preppies, led to no friendships. I came to and went from rehearsals as I did everything else that first year: by myself.

I have no doubt that being such a loner helped me survive the horrors of that year. Being alone, like not talking in class, avoided occasions for comparison and evaluation, but solitude extracted its price. I had no way of knowing, of course, that my worries about grades and anxiety about losing my scholarship, which required a B average to be renewed, were not unique. Neither were my fears of being exposed as an admissions committee mistake. I had no idea that others might be just as anxious.

I threw myself into my courses that first semester, discovering that as long as I avoided talking about the material in discussion sections or with friends outside of class, I was caught up in what I was learning and eager to go to lectures and do the reading. The world of ideas was opening up for me, and it seemed that its first chapter in every course was Plato. I read *The Republic* in Introduction to Western Political Theory, in Government 1, and in my great books course, Humanities 5. I knew Millis High was a world away in freshman composition when I had to write a paper every week and our graduate student instructor found sexual symbols in every text we read. "Yes, Hemingway's sun also rises," he quipped, "but Jake Barnes's doesn't."

I enjoyed the theater of the large lecture and was lucky in first term to have three superb masters of the art. My political theory professor was William Yandell Elliott, a towering six foot six with a barrel chest, big face, and dark, bushy eyebrows. A southern conservative from Virginia, Elliott had attended Vanderbilt and become one of the agrarian critics of liberalism, the "fugitives," that included John Crowe Ransom, Allen Tate, and Robert Penn Warren. After a Rhodes scholarship at Balliol College, Oxford, he was hired by A. Lawrence Lowell and had been at Harvard ever since. He was an advisor to several US presidents and served as the vice president of the War Production Board in World War II. Back at Harvard, he became the graduate mentor of Henry Kissinger, and when I arrived, in the fall of 1955, both were conservative faculty favorites. Elliott was a dramatic speaker, slowly making his arguments, which always ended in the Cold War division of all Western political thought into two camps. One, the totalitarian, ran from Plato to Stalin; the other, the free, ran from Aristotle to America. His height, girth, and melodramatic manner made him easy to parody, which we loved to do, especially his eagerly awaited goose-step promenade across the stage of Lowell lecture hall as he described fascism. In his lecture on Burke, Elliott quoted the manager of his Virginia estate to prove that deference to one's betters is natural and right. We also mimicked his southern drawl as he praised his faithful family retainer for acknowledging that he was truly a less worthy person than the great and good Professor Elliott.

In Natural Sciences 3, Harvard's General Education Committee tried to engage and inform the scientifically impaired or uninterested through a survey of the history of science, which began, of course, with Plato. The professor was I. Bernard Cohen, the distinguished historian of science. Educated at Harvard as an undergraduate and graduate student, Cohen was the biographer of Isaac Newton. A born showman, he easily satisfied the first commandment of college lecturing—"Thou shall not put your students to sleep"—while knocking basic science into our humanistic heads. Late in the semester, he ended the lecture on jet propulsion by nonchalantly placing his substantial and always well-tailored body on a worker's trolley, releasing a fire extinguisher, and propelling himself rapidly out the side door of Allston Burr lecture hall, opened with not a second to spare by his lab assistant.

The last of my trio of fabulous freshman lecturers, Henry Aiken, the philosopher who taught Humanities 5, was from the romantic school of lecturing, heartfelt and melodramatic. Aiken would leave

Harvard ten years later for a professorship at Brandeis, complaining that Harvard was too concerned with graduate education to the neglect of its undergraduates. He walked us through Hume or Hegel in carefully paced lectures, beginning softly and slowly before reaching a crescendo of flamboyant explosions. Utterly spent, he rushed out of the Emerson lecture room to recover with a cigarette by the water fountain in the hall. If you wanted to discuss something from the lecture with Professor Aiken, you waited by the fountain and caught him between puffs. Not that I ever did.

Elliott's course on political theory confirmed my resolve to major in government and set me on the path to an academic career. Playing a crucial role was my "section man," one of the young instructors who led discussions twice a week for about fifteen students in Elliott's class. A tall, twinkly-eyed man who did not look very Harvard, Al Mavrinac was uncommonly warm and kind in the classroom. His section, to which I was randomly assigned, was informative, peaceful, and fun, an oasis in noisy Harvard Square, much like the Radcliffe Quad itself, where he taught his class. Although I enjoyed Mr. Mavrinac's sections and his conservative politics, which were shaped by Catholicism (not Virginia and Balliol), I was still not inclined to speak in his classroom. He respected my silence, and I emerged from anonymity only when the time came to write my first term paper.

From the list of topics he circulated, I chose to write on "Plato, Locke, and Marx on private property." Having absolutely no idea how to write a college essay, I sought the advice of a Harvard sophomore, Howard Erdman, from Medway, the town next to Millis, whose name had been given to me by someone from my school. The son of a Jewish cantor, which provided us certain common interests, Howard was, more importantly, a government major. Graciously, he initiated me into the mysteries of the academic essay, which involved, he told me, offering my readings of the three theorists as reorganized renderings of Elliott's lectures and Mavrinac's section notes, supplemented by as many secondary sources on Plato, Locke, and Marx as I could find.

Erdman, who would become a professor of political science at Dartmouth, also taught me the value of taking a provocative position, especially one contrary to the professor's. This approach, he insisted, guaranteed a good grade, since no faculty member wanted to appear biased in his grading. I took his advice and suggested at the end of my paper that there was little to recommend Locke's theory of private property over the collectivism of Plato and Marx and that it was impossible to find one tradition morally superior to the other. It worked. Mavrinac returned the paper with a good grade and an unusual, if anguished, comment: "I disagree and so would most priests, ministers, and rabbis, but so be it."

That I opportunistically set aside my still strongly felt conservative convictions, forged by Millis and the American Legion, reveals how terrified I was about not doing well and losing my scholarship. I took scrupulously detailed lecture notes in all my courses, lest I miss anything that might appear on an exam, and I did all my reading on time, often working late into the night.

When the first exam period came in mid-January, I was terrified that I would be unable to write an exam for three hours. I studied methodically with a system I used for the rest of college: I reduced class and reading notes to consecutively smaller numbers of 3 × 5 cards until the night before the exam, when the course would be reduced to one card on which the basic themes of the course were distilled. I tried to get a good night's sleep and always put the card with the keys to the course by my pillow as if some process of osmosis would fix it in my head. On exam day, unshaven and in the same clothes worn for each exam day, I went to the cavernous Memorial Hall, the site of most finals, where, if at all possible, I sat so I was looking at a nearby wall and not at row after row of other students taking tests at their desks. I survived the exams with my nervousness gone by the end of the first hour. After the semester's last exam was over, I got drunk for the first time in my life on cheap gin and orange juice shared with my roommates. Like other students, I put postcards in my blue examination books so that instructors would mail the final grade. When the postcards arrived, I learned I had done fine in my first semester, which I attributed, of course, to having studied harder and longer than my less-worried classmates.

Two nonacademic freshman requirements contributed to the general misery of that first year: passing my swimming test and my campus job. Two days a week I trudged down Holyoke Street to the IAB, the Indoor Athletic Building, whose many plaques suggested that it was only there that Teddy Roosevelt spent his Harvard years. I had hated swimming ever since I almost drowned the summer Helen had me take lessons on a pond in Natick. Nonetheless, since all Harvard freshmen had to pass a swimming test, my physical education course prepared me for my prelim in the pool. I disliked getting undressed and wet on a cold winter day as well as the humiliation at my inability to improve as the year wore on. I passed, finally, but only because the instructors stretched the rules to allow me to do the required distance floating on my back.

My campus job at the graduate dining hall, located beyond the law school in a set of buildings designed by Walter Gropius with Miró paintings on the wall, and for which I received the grand sum of $300, was boring and time consuming. I worked the lunch shift on Mondays, Wednesdays, and Fridays all year, always at the condiment section of the food line, where, among other duties, I made the Russian dressing. By midyear, the thought of mixing large vats of mayonnaise and ketchup revolted me. Far from building character, working in the dining hall was tedious and tiring, even if it did lead to a brief conversation with Eleanor Roosevelt. Passing through the line one day, the former first lady asked me most politely the whereabouts of the Italian dressing, an encounter that in later years I would shamelessly recast for my children as "Have I told you about the time I had a talk with Eleanor Roosevelt?"

As hellish as freshman year was, it was also an exhilarating, emancipatory experience, as residential college life has become in American culture for those who can afford it or who, like me, have scholarships. Liberated from family and hometown, I was free to eat, sleep, study, and socialize if or when I wanted to. For me, especially when I was feeling blue, this freedom meant exploring Harvard Square at any time, day or night. It wasn't Millis. I discovered coffee at Albioni's and especially Hayes-Bickford, where Alfred North Whitehead's eccentric daughter often sat with a parrot on her shoulder. I discovered dirty paperbacks at Kahaly's, the magazine store then next to J. August's. I added professors to my spotting efforts, thrilled when I spied the walrus-looking Roscoe

Pound, retired dean of the law school and eminent legal theorist, coming out of the Harvard Coop. Harvard Square's landmark eatery, Elsie's, with its famous roast beef sandwich, was, of course, off limits for an observant Jew like me, and I was too much the loner to drink beer at Cronin's or see many movies at the Brattle Theater, activities that in my mind required company.

Acting in our parents' place, *in loco parentis*, Harvard encouraged this transition to freedom and maturity through traditional rites of passage like the annual Freshman Smoker. How better to celebrate surviving the first semester than to start the second with a giant beer party in Memorial Hall? The floor was so covered with brew after an hour that a sloshed frosh like me could make a running slide to greet a smiling F. Skiddy von Stade Jr., who, unlikely as it seems in light of contemporary attitudes toward college drinking, was belting them down as determinedly as we were. To my amazement, this ramrod-straight, three-piece-suited super WASP shared his life story with two other freshmen and with me. He had grown up in Old Westbury on Long Island in the world of *The Great Gatsby*. He prepped at St. Paul's School in New Hampshire and then went to Harvard, class of 1938, arriving with two polo ponies. He stayed at Harvard as an administrator, he told us, because he loved it, and his only other passion was in professional polo competition. I was dazzled, but in the more sober light of the next day, I was somewhat appalled; WASP envy was complicated, riven as it was with streams of love and hate.

After the smoker and Skiddy, my besotted freshman class went next door to Sanders Theater for a variety show with Al Capp, the short, misanthropic *Li'l Abner* cartoonist, as master of ceremonies. Halfway through the show, Capp became so angry at the obscenities the future leaders of America shouted at him that he walked out and returned to the serenity of his Brattle Street home. Such were the initiations to manhood for the elite at midcentury, and such were my joyous respites from the hell of freshman year.

I spent my upper-class years at Winthrop House alongside the Charles River, which served as a constant reminder of where I'd come from, its waters upstream marking the Millis-Medfield boundary. I picked Winthrop because Mr. Mavrinac, who would go on to a long career at Colby, was its senior tutor and lived there with his wife, who taught at Wellesley. I didn't really care that it was the jock house or that Joe Kennedy's boys, including Jack, then the sitting senator from Massachusetts, had lived there. Winthrop was a self-contained community of 350 sophomores, juniors, and seniors and nearly twenty affiliated faculty, with its own library, common room, and dining hall. The jocks were a raucous presence in Winthrop—both the "animals," as we labeled the friendly football players from nearby Somerville or the faraway Pennsylvania coalfields, and the only slightly more refined hockey players like Bill Cleary. They obeyed the letter of Harvard's rule requiring ties and jackets at meals but wore them over tee shirts or, on occasion, naked chests. At Saturday night dinner, one of the "animals" invariably smashed the Gropius-designed hard round plastic food tray, ubiquitous in Harvard dining halls, over the head of an equally inebriated friend (never, thank goodness, on the head of a non-jock nearby). Despite the omnipresent jocks, the overall tone of the house was warm and friendly, a mood set by its Anglophilic master, the historian of philanthropy and of Britain David Owen, and Al Mavrinac. Winthrop was neither aggressively intellectual like Eliot House next door on the river or snobbishly aloof like Lowell House, behind us and across the street.

In this congenial house community, I reverted to the social self I crafted in high school, no doubt helped by no longer worrying about flunking out or losing my scholarship. I made many friends, mostly Jewish, I realize in retrospect. It seemed easier. Some were cultivated, refined, and soft spoken, a kind of Jew I'd hardly met before. A few of these Winthrop House friends, like Guido Goldman—son of Nachum Goldman, president of the World Zionist Organization, "King of the Jews," we called him—Pete Edelman, and Bob Rubin went on to distinction and fame, though I have stayed in touch with none of them. Goldman, from New York City, would negotiate the German Marshall Fund with the German government and be its first director as well as the director of Harvard's Center for European Studies. Edelman, from Minneapolis, would become a law professor at Georgetown and then work for the Clinton administration. He resigned his position to protest Clinton's signing welfare reform legislation. Rubin, from Miami, would become a major force on Wall Street and ultimately secretary of the treasury for President Clinton.

But most of my closest friends were poorer, unsophisticated Jews like me, from the Boston area, whose parents had not gone to college. My circle included Boston Latin School graduates who hung out at Dudley House, the commuter center, like Arnie Miller, whose mother and father owned a small variety store in Brighton. Senior year, Arnie roomed with me in Winthrop House. Slowly I left my self-constructed shell, though still keeping up with my schoolwork and studying hard for exams. I played poker and whist and went to football games, Cronin's, and movies at the Brattle with friends. I joined the Gilbert and Sullivan Players and sang in the chorus in productions of *Patience* and *Trial by Jury*. Finally, I was on the stage.

While I became more sociable, intellectually I remained a loner. My friends were not intellectual mates; we did things together or talked about life, people, and politics, but, by my choice, seldom about ideas, books we read, or courses we took. As an upperclassman, I still found it difficult to expose myself intellectually in face-to-face exchanges, remained silent in class, and studied alone in my room.

Sociable though I was, I spent most of my time with Boston buddies and seldom dated. Radcliffe girls frightened me with their intellectuality and social cool, as did the coeds from Wellesley and Smith who were imported en masse on weekends. I seldom talked before or after class with a "Cliffie." The few girls I dated were from Boston University, Simmons, or neighboring Leslie College—girls, as Helen might put it, more "within my element." But as a Harvard man, I was as awkward and shy with them as I had been at AZA-BBG dances. On Saturdays my buddies and I watched the couples at Winthrop's date night dinner with envy and resentment before we left for Cronin's and beer. One girl did call me occasionally. Nancy Simon, a student from Boston University, who came from Franklin near Millis and whose mother was active in Helen's Hadassah chapter, dropped by Cambridge every now and then, once to visit me at Stillman Infirmary where I was laid up with mononucleosis, but more often to have coffee and hang out. Fond of opera, she seemed much too worldly for me, but I had a crush on her. After a while it became clear that she had a crush on Harvard, not me.

Life improved on the job front, too, after freshman year. As I learned how things worked at Harvard and how to serve my own interests, the jobs got better. Howard Erdman was my guide here as well. He introduced me to Mr. Connors, another Medway man, who assigned work to scholarship students. Mr. Connors got easy jobs for me each year that allowed me to study a good part of the time I was on the clock. One year I signed people in at the squash courts (then in the triangle between Kirkland, Eliot, and Winthrop Houses). When I wasn't studying, I learned to play squash, thus earning credentials as an ersatz WASP, well on my way to being an Ivy League gentleman. In the following two years, courtesy of the Medway-Millis mafia, I was on the payroll as night watchman at Holyoke House, the building on Mass Avenue then housing the government and economics tutorial offices, where I sat at the head of a long stairway keeping track of the very few faculty and students who came by, getting paid mainly for studying.

While I took Harvard in stride after freshman year and felt sufficiently confident to allow my sociable, card-playing, Cronin's-drinking self to reemerge, I was also forging a new post-Millis self in which I enjoyed my academic work, studying hard not simply to get good grades so I could be secretary of state or, as Helen now urged, a rich lawyer but because I liked immersing myself in the world of ideas for its own sake. I was becoming a biographical cliché: the unreflective, instrumental kid turned on to ideas, culture, and the life of the mind by college. I was succumbing to what the writer Leon Wieseltier has described as "the charisma of the intellect."

Two Harvard professors became my guides on this journey. Stanley Hoffmann and Judith Shklar, my mentors and role models, were in their late twenties and were themselves close friends. They would go on to distinguished careers at Harvard and as internationally renowned writers on politics. Hoffmann and Shklar were Europeans who had fled fascism and embraced the American ideal of meritocracy. I benefitted from their commitment to it, since I seemed proof to them that anyone, even a Jewish country bumpkin in foster care, could make it at Harvard. Hoffmann, a bachelor at the time, lived in Winthrop House and led the sophomore tutorial I took with five other government majors. Once a week we'd meet in the sitting room of his suite with its leather chairs and Oriental rugs and discuss classic texts in social and political theory like Alexis de Toqueville's *Democracy in America*. I was the quietest of the sextet, though.

I made up for my reticence at meals, which is where my relationship with Hoffmann flourished. He ate most of his meals in Winthrop House, and when I joined him, which I often did, the informality of the setting emboldened me to speak. Hoffman was at his best at breakfast, to which he came at exactly 8:16 am, right after the CBS radio morning news, always stimulated by recent events. These were magical meals, the conversation roaming everywhere, led by his interest in everything.

Over coffee after dinner Hoffmann opened up the world of culture for me, introducing me particularly to film as art, with insightful analyses of *The Grand Illusion* or Bergman's latest at the Brattle. He showed me how to view film and theatre as social commentary. I was, for example, unabashedly excited with a Harvard production of *Death of a Salesman*, the first serious play I'd ever seen. I saw it as a powerful story about the dynamics of one American family, with Willy Loman seeming much like Saul. Hoffmann, however, revealed Miller's more general concerns with the values of postwar America. He was always gentle and supportive at the table and in tutorial, seldom judgmental or critical. I was starstruck, in awe of his learning, his French wit, and his kindness, and deeply touched that he liked me. I wanted to be just like him.

In junior year, government majors moved on to one-on-one faculty tutorials, and Hoffmann arranged for me to be assigned to Judith Shklar. Mrs. Shklar, as everyone then called her, was one of the very few women on the Harvard faculty. She was married to a professor of dentistry at Tufts and had two young sons when I met her for weekly tutorials on eighteenth-century political thought at 4:30 pm in her office at Apley Court, a part of Dudley House. I had never met anyone who talked as fast as she did, and she told me she had never met a Harvard undergraduate who dressed as gauchely and seemed as provincial as I did. I no longer can recall from those

tutorials her observations on Voltaire, Montesquieu, or Godwin, but
I have never forgotten my wonder at the play of her mind, nor have
I forgotten the exuberance and excitement with which she intro-
duced me to ideas and to history.

I was tense and frightened on those afternoons; she did not suf-
fer fools gladly. But I walked back to Winthrop House in the winter
darkness exhilarated, my head spinning. Mrs. Shklar was my guide
to a world that became my professional home. I would not have
entered it without her nor stayed long in it without her encour-
agement. She was so much like the people she taught me about,
the giants of the eighteenth-century Enlightenment. Skeptical to
the core, suspicious of cant, enthusiasm, and excess, she humbled
anyone who claimed to have found absolute truth, especially if this
truth was forced on others. She could be very tough and she could
be very caring. Along with the tutorials, I remember the warm welcome of evenings at her home, where she and Gerry, her husband,
opened my ears to great music and my eyes to great art. The dinners she served me were emblems of the nurturance and respect
she gave me. I was too thin, she always insisted.

This transformation was marked by the pleasure I found in writing as an upperclassman and the personal significance writing came
to have for me. I associate these feelings with the first serious piece
of writing I did at Harvard, a paper for Arthur Schlesinger Jr.'s course
on American intellectual history.

Typically anonymous among its three hundred undergraduates, I
loved Schlesinger's course, marveling at the brilliance of the lectures
despite the odd grimace with which he punctuated his enunciation
of words in an otherwise immobile face. It was a treat to be in the
presence of one of America's great historians. But I felt in this class
a sense of being an outsider at Harvard, never far from the surface,
since after every lecture the short bow-tied professor walked off
with John Fell Stevenson, the son of Adlai Stevenson, and Elizabeth
Niebuhr, the daughter of Reinhold Niebuhr. Seeing this trio, we
would quip "there goes the ADA," since along with the parents of
the two students Schlesinger had founded the liberal, anti-communist Americans for Democratic Action. Forty-five years later I had
the privilege of introducing Professor Schlesinger, who was speaking

to an American studies conference in Turin, Italy, where I told this story of the ritualistic ending of his lectures. Schlesinger, then in his eighties, was sitting behind me ready to come to the podium, so I couldn't see him as I spoke. My wife, Miriam, later told me that tears came to his eyes as I reminisced about his lectures.

A twenty-page paper was required in Schlesinger's course, and from the list of topics provided I chose to write on Whittaker Chambers, the editor of *Time* magazine and accuser of Alger Hiss, who in his book *Witness* had described his commitment to communism, his break from it, and then his fierce, some might say fanatical, religiously based anti-communism. Schlesinger had not lectured on Chambers, and the book was too new to have created a stir or articles and books assessing it. The cut-and-paste approach to writing papers, which I had learned from Howard Erdman, wouldn't work. All I could do was read Chambers's book. I did and I outlined the paper's argument—my own argument, not the arguments of others. What I wrote is by now an academic truism, and even then, I later found out, such arguments were being made by others. But it was an act of discovery and creativity for me at the time. I suggested that Chambers, an intelligent and sensitive person, had become a communist for the very reasons he later left the party and became a religious anti-communist zealot. He was on a quest for an all-encompassing set of beliefs whose doctrinal simplicity and authoritative repudiation of alternatives provided certainty. The teaching assistant for the course, Nat Huggins, later a distinguished scholar of the Harlem Renaissance, liked the paper so much he showed it to Professor Schlesinger, who commended it as well.

This writing experience helped change me and my sense of self. Still consumed with feelings of inferiority alongside classmates from Choate, Groton, Boston Latin, Exeter, Stuyvesant, Shaker Heights, and Horace Mann and still reluctant to speak in class, I discovered that writing was a way to assert myself, to confront others, to put myself forward. Writing was private. I wrote in my room, and my essays were read and evaluated when I wasn't present. I was less immediately exposed in writing, the potential ridicule distanced. And so, through writing, I made my mark at Harvard. Professors liked my papers and I got good grades. Putting myself forward in

writing, doing it well, and being noticed validated me, literally seeming to give value to myself.

I never then—and seldom now, a half century later—conceived
of the life of the mind as verbal agon. I am a disputative and sometimes controversial scholar, but I still assert myself principally in the
relative safety of writing, not in conference panels or roundtables.
This dimension of writing, its privacy, may be central to understanding the role and significance of writing for many people. It certainly
is in my case.

In the course of my intellectual awakening at Harvard I went
through a spiritual crisis, just as my foster mother and my high
school teachers had predicted. I didn't yet become an atheist, as
many nineteenth-century sons of Harvard apparently did. But I
became less religious. My faith was shaken, as I have told generations of students, by Hume, Freud, and Bacon. Hume's essay on
miracles in Henry Aiken's Humanities 5 and then Freud's psycho-
analytic reading of religion in *Future of an Illusion* convinced me
that prayer and *frumkeit* (piety) defied reason. The effect of texts
like these and, I have to add, the long walk to Hillel was my abandonment of Hillel's Shabbos services. By freshman year's second
semester I stopped my three or four kosher dinners a week at Hillel.
And then there's bacon, not Sir Francis, but swine. One Sunday
in May I ate bacon at the Freshman Union and wondered how a
good God could forbid such deliciousness. There was no real spiritual crisis, no anguishing over a loss of faith, since my religiosity
was never faith based but rooted in the security of repetitive ritual. When *frumkeit* is understood to be irrational, the end comes
easily. Unlike the nineteenth-century Harvard men, I did little soul
searching and had no regrets.

I felt no decline in Jewish identity, however; my self-identifying
pride was enhanced, in fact, by the realization that Freud, Einstein,
Marx, and so many other giants I read about freshman year were
Jewish. I forged in college a more intellectual or quasi-political
identification of *Yiddishkeit* with the prophetic quest for *tikkun*,
for "repairing the world," for seeking social justice, though a part
of me always linked Jewishness and its symbolic representation in
food and music with the warm embrace of childhood.

Fig. 12 | Isaac receiving award at the American Legion–sponsored Massachusetts Boys State, Amherst, MA

I was moving left as well, though by no means as far as my Millis teachers had predicted. My political transformation lacks, alas, the specific benchmarks of the religious. In Hoffmann's sophomore tutorial I was the only Republican, hoping Eisenhower would defeat Stevenson. But by senior year I considered myself a liberal and a Democrat. More important than reading and explaining my post-Millis politics was the influence of my teachers. Hoffmann and Shklar were levelheaded liberals as well as secular Jews, and other than Elliott and Mavrinac, most of my best teachers were liberals. Schlesinger was soon to go to Washington with Kennedy; H. Stuart Hughes, whose European intellectual history course I took, would run for the US Senate as an anti-nuclear advocate; and Sam Beer, who taught me about British politics, was a government professor quite visible in liberal circles.

It was hard to resist the gentleman's liberalism that pervaded Harvard then, which expressed itself in a knee-jerk anti-Catholicism

Fig. 13 | Isaac as a counselor at Boys State

or in elitist disdain for both the "organization man" and "the lonely crowd," impulses I then found congenial, especially when joined to the conviction that liberals could rid the world of poverty, ignorance, and injustice. When I left Millis for Cambridge that September, I left my American Legion speech behind, the first time I had done so. Harvard was transforming me, to be sure, but parts of Millis stayed with me. I continued to feel ambivalent about a life focused on ideas. Intellectuals struck me as pretentious, self-important, and arrogant. Most importantly, I couldn't rid myself of the gut feeling that intellectuals didn't really work for a living. Sometimes I found studying or writing in my room, and the whole enterprise of the university seemed so disconnected from real life that I'd get up early and wander through Harvard Square at six or seven in the morning, just to see real people getting on and off buses and scurrying off to real work. Harvard had its aesthetes and intellectuals in the 1950s, but my friends were not intellectuals, nor did they consider me one, even though some of us were considering academic careers. Such was the mood of America in the Eisenhower era, even at Harvard.

None of the transformations I was undergoing made it easy when I went back to Millis on weekends or vacations. Like many undergraduates, I went home frequently freshman year and less often as an upperclassman. I still went to shul if I were there on Shabbos or *yontifs* (holidays), though more for the pleasures of Nelly's home than for religion's sake; if I were given an *aliyah* I felt very much the impostor. I was deeply divided in Millis for, on the one hand, these were the "real" people I sought in my early morning forays into Harvard Square, but I increasingly found them boring and provincial. Helen and Saul continued to fight, and their conversations seldom went deeper than the prices of lettuce in the Stop and Shop and the A&P. Helen talked about a former schoolmate or old friend of mine she'd run into, but I kept to myself, doing my college reading or wandering the fields and pastures. I hoped Helen and Saul or one of the Maels would ask about my studies or notice the changes in me, but they never did.

Things were not much different when my foster parents visited me in Cambridge, which Helen, much more than Saul, loved to do. I was surprised and ashamed at how embarrassed I was by them, even though my roommates and friends relished the homemade fudge and pastries Helen brought. Even the care packages were part of the problem. I could understand Helen and Saul's inability to appreciate my schoolwork, but I would have liked overt expressions of interest and affection toward me. What I got, instead, were injunctions to put on more weight and date more. The goodies, I suspected, were stand-ins for nurturance and love, which also provided Helen intense satisfaction, as she insistently asked which of my friends had liked which pastry. She reminded me of Max, who had substituted money and candy for love. At the same time, I must have seemed a different person to Helen and Saul, uncommunicative and sullen, easily angered. I spoke back when Helen found something to criticize, even if it was the truth about my disorderly room. I am sure my embarrassment and lack of appreciation were evident and hurtful to them.

We now lived in different worlds and spoke in different languages, a development, I suppose, not that unusual when children
of uneducated parents go to college. Complicating the problem in
our case was Helen's fear that after college I would go my own way
and have nothing to do with her. In truth, I was becoming increasingly uncertain about my identification as their son and did not
know how I would—or should—treat the Spiros after graduation.
So I kept my emotional distance on these reunions, which probably
made matters worse. After they left Cambridge or when I returned
from Millis, I went through the same ritual to calm down. I played
Mozart's flute concertos on the small stereo I had bought in Harvard
Square, almost as a sign of who I now was, even as I felt pangs of
guilt for leaving behind where I had come from and who I had been.

I heard from my social worker that Helen worried that I might
establish a relationship with Max, even though he had not congrat-
ulated me on graduating from high school or on being admitted
to Harvard. In fact, I had no interest in seeing Max, who never
visited me at Harvard. But I did see a lot of my social worker, Mr.
Warschauer, in my first year. He came to Harvard about every two
months to see how I was doing. He reassured me that the state would
give me extra money for clothes that year and described when and
how decisions on continued support would be made. Concerned
about my anxiety, Mr. Warschauer set up an appointment for the
two of us with Wallace Macdonald, who told me that I should not
worry about my scholarship renewal.

At the beginning of my sophomore year, I mentioned in passing
to Mr. Warschauer that it was inconvenient to borrow other students' typewriters, which I had done freshman year, for I now had
many more papers to write. Sure enough, several weeks later I was
sent a typewriter as a gift from Judge Harry Stone of the Probate
Court of Plymouth County, who had learned about me from the
head social worker of the Division of Child Guardianship.

As helpful as Mr. Warschauer was, I was not all that fond of him.
He offered what he thought was useful advice on dating, study habits, and cultivating a moral character, always delivered in a tone
reflecting envy and disdain for the Ivy League and a smug sense
that he was the font of wisdom and experience. By the middle of

sophomore year we agreed that I would keep in touch mainly by letter. He promised, in turn, to handle financial details, like Harvard's
medical insurance, from his Brockton office. I initiated the new
arrangements, evidence, I think, of a greater sense of self-confi-
dence, and, probably because I found his visits and advice tedious,
reflecting as well a sense of intellectual superiority vis-à-vis a dull
government functionary. My arrogance, transparent and hurtful,
led the following year to an unpleasant and unexpected confron-
tation between me and the state.

Its source was my sudden desire to learn more about my family
history, which I had previously resisted. Reading Freud's *Introductory
Lectures on Psychoanalysis* my junior year, with its claims about the
importance of the infant's relationship to the mother, I sought for
the first time to know the details of my life before Millis. I asked
Mr. Warschauer to bring my file to Cambridge. He replied that I
should come to his Brockton office to read it, pointing out that it
was unusual, if not illegal, to show me the case record. Best, therefore, that it remain in the office. I replied that such a trip, involving
a subway ride to Quincy and then a train ride to Brockton, was too
time-consuming. He held fast, so I gave in, only to cancel several
appointments at the last minute in the face of deadlines for papers
and impending exams. One cancellation particularly upset him
because he had arranged for me to meet Judge Stone when I came
to Brockton. I finally went to Brockton after Mr. Warschauer wrote
that cancelling appointments might jeopardize my board and clothing allowance renewal for senior year, since the state saw it as part
of "a pattern of Isaac wanting things to be done for him."

In his office, on his own turf, and before discussing my family history, Mr. Warschauer lectured me on the need to show more
appreciation to the state. My aloofness in the past few months, he
added, left him and his colleagues wondering if their unusual invest-
ment in me had been justified.

I had a lengthy discussion with Isaac about his feelings toward
DCG. I did point out to Isaac the importance of careful thinking in regard to his relationship to others particularly authority
figures as represented by the DCG. Since he is in the field of

Government I suggested to him that this would be important to him. I then discussed with him the need of his understanding of the DCG and suggested that it would be very helpful to the department should this understanding be more prevalent.

Surprised that the state sounded so much like Helen in its eagerness to be thanked for its role in shaping me and very much wanting to move on to why I had come, I responded that "I was grateful toward the Division of Child Guardianship because of the help it has given me, but I am the kind of person who does not show such feelings." The file entry for the visit concludes:

After this I asked Isaac whether he was still interested in learning about his background and he said that he was. I discussed with him his family difficulties and his mother's hospitalization. Isaac was quite interested in this although some of the matters which were discussed may have produced feelings on his part he seemed to handle them quite well and seemed understanding of the situation as it was. He also was very much interested in his own placements and I discussed these with him. At the end of the evening I felt that a good deal had been accomplished. This was both in terms of a mutual understanding and discussion of Isaac's own family background. He looked very well and seemed to have gained weight. I feel that he is maturing quite well.

Indeed, a good deal had been accomplished, and I did handle it well. I mulled it over on the long train and subway ride back to Cambridge, less the lecture on gratitude than the details of my first five years. I had known, vaguely, about my mother and her death in 1952 from Max's postcard to Helen, "Please tell Isaac that his mother died," but never the details of her illness and confinement. It was the first time I'd ever heard about Mrs. Milford, Mrs. Perricotte, and Mrs. Bell.

I told no one about my odyssey to Brockton, certainly not Helen, and ruminated on my discovery for days in long solitary walks through Harvard Square and along the Charles River. Running through my mind was one of Mr. Warschauer's recurring questions

Fig. 14 | Isaac off to Harvard

from freshman year. Did I think, he had asked, that my feelings of inferiority had anything to do with my family background? I thought of the question in the wake of the trip to Brockton, because what I felt emerging was not a sense of inferiority but paradoxically a sense of pride, especially in light of my Freud readings, a pride in my own accomplishments, my resiliency, and my capacity to create myself and not be beholden to either Helen or the state. That I had navigated through and survived a deprived childhood, I realized, was at the core of a proud sense of self. Alas, with that pride came some feelings of moral superiority to those with conventional childhoods and untroubled pasts or those who, from my perspective, had much less serious traumas like mean parents or sibling rivals.

By a kind of unspoken mutual understanding, Mr. Warschauer and I had no contact with each other my senior year, my last in state custody, for in March 1959 I turned twenty-one. I was preoccupied most of the year with my senior honors thesis, under Mrs. Shklar's supervision, on the political thought of William Godwin, the English Enlightenment's anarchist theorist. Each day and most evenings in my room, I wrote and revised, drawing on the eighteenth-century texts I'd borrowed from Widener Library. I enjoyed research so much that I began to have intimations of a calling, a life of the mind as exemplified by my mentor, Mrs. Shklar. To make me culturally literate, she advised a yearlong history of art course. Because it was taught at midday with many slides, we called it "darkness at noon," or, more cleverly, "from clay to Klee." To open my mind beyond Europe, she suggested "rice paddies," the yearlong survey of East Asian civilization taught by the eminent duo of John King Fairbank and Edwin O. Reischauer. I took all her advice, thinking at some point that I might pursue professionally the social and political history of art in graduate school.

Whether I would apply to graduate school or law school was the dilemma of early senior year, and I decided to defer the decision until spring. Helen assumed I was going to be a lawyer, while Mrs. Shklar was convinced I should be a professor. I voted with my wrist: I got roaring drunk the night before my Law School Aptitude Test, abandoning my rigorous regime before exams. This subconscious decision to sabotage law school was rooted in a sense that lawyering required the verbal agon and in-your-face competitiveness with which I had difficulty. Working away at my senior thesis, I realized that an academic career allowed for, indeed required, long periods of solitude. Writing provided a subtler, less scary kind of competitiveness, which I could deal with and perhaps even thrive on.

While I wrote the senior thesis, I managed to spend a lot of time with my friends, who were also trying to sort out their ambitions to be doctors, lawyers, professors, clergy, and businessmen. Like me, they were surprised when late on a winter night someone slipped

a letter under my door with the news that I had been selected for
Phi Beta Kappa as one of the "senior sixteen," along with the explanation that at the end of junior year eight from our class had been
chosen, now sixteen, with another eighty or so to be added at graduation. The next day I discovered that the previous night a number
of seniors who, unlike me, knew all about PBK had stayed up watching the threshold below their suite doors.

My Harvard years ended with a bundle of wonderful developments. My thesis won a department prize, I was awarded a Harvard
Knox traveling fellowship to spend a year at England's Cambridge
University, and I graduated summa cum laude. Still, I never took
myself that seriously as an intellectual—to wit, the comedy of errors
on graduation day. On that hot Thursday in the middle of June, with
the tension behind me of finding Helen and Saul a parking place and
seats between Widener's steps and Memorial Church, I marched to
Harvard Yard from Winthrop House with my class of '59 contingent,
joking that Big Brother might ban our twenty-fifth reunion in 1984.
Entering the Yard, I was grabbed by one of the score of Harvard
"baby" deans, or "deanlets," as we sometimes called them. He'd been
looking for me because all the other summas were marching at the
head of the class, not with their house buddies, and I hadn't gotten
the notice. His crimson gown flapping away, he hustled me to the
designated spot in the Yard where I was supposed to be, a fitting
footnote to four years at Harvard, still being slightly out of place.

That spring, the Commonwealth of Massachusetts ended twenty-one years of benevolent care with comparable drama—not with
a bang nor even a whimper. There was no visit, no call, not even
a letter, nor one from me to them. We had burned our bridges at
Brockton. There is the last line in my file:

*4/10/59. (CASE CLOSED.) ISAAC KRAMNICK, VILLAGE STREET, MIL-
LIS. DISCHARGED TO SELF.*

AFTERWORD: THE BROTHERS K

Life after Harvard has been very good. Since that last entry in my file, #24269, that "self" has done quite well. "Discharged to self," I have "made it," have lived a version of the American dream: from humble, disadvantaged origins to what most people would deem success. I move rapidly now through these decades, to bookend this description of my years as a foster child, and to finish the story of my brothers Sigmund and Leon, we three Brothers K.

The year at Cambridge University was followed by graduate school, again at Harvard and again with the inimitable mentorship of Judith Shklar. And I have been in academic life ever since, teaching for several years at Brandeis and Yale and, since 1972, at Cornell. Cornell has suited me perfectly; it is the most egalitarian, the least stuffy of the Ivy League schools, a world-class Ivy with a Big Ten soul. I have made my mark as a professor, author, and editor of over a score of books, have been elected a member of the prestigious American Academy of Arts and Sciences and England's Royal Historical Society, have served Cornell in many administrative positions, and, of most importance to me, have been recognized as a well-loved teacher.

I have had a happy, love-filled marriage for fifty years, a marvelous life gift, given the dysfunctional model provided by Helen and Saul. In graduate school I met my partner in loving friendship and intellectual companionship, the teacher and writer Miriam Brody, and we have produced three delightful and interesting children, a daughter who is a lawyer, another who is a social worker / therapist, and a son who is a college professor. And we have four grandchildren, the dessert of life.

Miriam and I met the summer of 1962, and we like to say it was Ted Kennedy who brought us together. We were both helping a Boston University political scientist, Murray Levin, do research on

Massachusetts voter attitudes toward the Democratic primary campaign for the US Senate between Ted, the young and inexperienced
brother of the president of the United States, and Eddy, the son of
John McCormack, the Speaker of the US House of Representatives.
Our job was to knock on doors in the Jamaica Plain section of Boston
and interview registered Democrats, a task made almost impossible because with the notorious Boston Strangler on the loose, few
people were inclined to open their doors. Our romance flourished,
nevertheless, in our frustrated careers as fledgling social scientists,
and that fall I brought Miriam to Millis for the first time. It blew
her mind, to use the vernacular of the 1960s. Brought up in a row
house in Philadelphia and in a secular urban Jewish environment,
she could not believe the time warp of Millis, the nineteenth-century European Jewish ghetto plunked down in its Norman Rockwell
Americana small-town setting. Helen hosted an engagement party
at our house, where, after meeting Miriam, a neighbor, Polly Rosen,
told everyone of Miriam's articulateness: "Poils came from her
mouth" (which I explained to Miriam was Yiddish-American for
"pearls came from her mouth"). To this day I occasionally resur-
rect Polly Rosen's observation in a private moment after Miriam
has said something particularly clever.

Life with Miriam and our children taught me how to love and
led me ultimately to make my peace with Helen. I continued to
regard Helen and Saul as parents, quite aware that this was a con-
scious choice. The Spiros, I realized, were my family, for better and
for worse. My feelings of filial affection were never intense, but having "parents" made marriage and parenthood seem easier, more
grounded, more "normal." Our relationship would not be very close,
however. Helen, though pleased Miriam was Jewish, never warmly
embraced her, in part because she was not Orthodox, and we did
not keep a kosher home or have a ritual circumcision for our son.
Nor did Helen give much love or attention to her grandchildren,
seldom hugging, kissing, or playing with them, expecting rather
that they be dutiful and respectful to her. She didn't consider me a
failure, always ready to wrap the copy of my latest book in plastic
before putting it beside the others on the table next to the TV. But
my professorial, nonmaterialistic style of life disappointed her, and

she constantly regaled me with descriptions of other people's gorgeous homes and expensive vacations.

On visits to Helen and Saul in Millis, I foolishly expected some loving interest in me and was invariably disappointed. Not that I was without fault. I was seldom affectionate or warm to Helen and never seemed to worry about her need for reassurance, gratitude, even love. We went through life unable to express how important each of us was to the other or give voice to unconditional love.

Saul remained unpleasant, vulgar, and filled with rage until the day he died in 1987. He spent his years before retirement in the textile mill doing backbreaking work, lifting and moving large bales of fabric. In retirement he spent the day at the dining room table playing solitaire. Still volatile, he might throw dishes on the floor or scream at Helen even when we visited with the children. But, unlike Helen, he sometimes tried to amuse his grandchildren, even if it involved, as it usually did, taking out and playing with his false teeth (which my kids loved, of course).

Zayde lived deep into his nineties, energetic and sharp to the end. On his deathbed he announced his preference for Stanetsky's funeral home over Schlossberg's and invoked the wrath of the eternal hereafter if his wishes were not followed. The next day the doors of his country shul were opened wide when the hearse took his body on its journey from his room at Nelly's house past his beloved shul and onto Route 109 and Stanetsky's in Boston. Presiding over the funeral was, of course, the Bostoner Rebbe.

I failed to keep up with most of the other Maels after Harvard. My "cousins" dispersed after Zayde's death; a few remained in Millis, while most moved to suburban Brookline and Brighton and others to New York City, New Jersey, Baltimore, and Chicago. Helen and Saul left Millis as well, moving to a garden court apartment in Stoughton, not far from the site of the Sharon Sanatorium of my boyhood. The shul in the field was sold and converted by its new owner into a private house. Virtually all the children of my cousins, and their children as well, went to college and are now part of the American Jewish success story, working as doctors, nurses, lawyers, rabbis, and sports announcers, with, I suspect, a good number of Democrats among them. Truly amazing, and not that typical, is that they remain deeply religious, virtually all of them, and each generation chooses Orthodox partners. The spirit of Zayde hovers still over his far-flung progeny.

I have returned to Millis several times for high school class reunions, usually dinners, which I, as senior class president, have to organize. Miriam generously comes along. An amazing twelve or thirteen of our original nineteen (after Dick Pixley's pre-graduation car death) usually show up. Gerry is an affable, joke-telling glad-hander; Shirley Spencer is a deeply believing Christian family farmer in Maine. Olga Maranjian is a professor of nursing and my cousin.

Marilyn doesn't come because the Millis Restaurant is not kosher. Everyone calls me Sonny, a name I abandoned after marriage, and Bill Keough, a well-to-do owner of an animal research lab, announced of Miriam at one early reunion, "Who would have thought Sonny would marry such a looker?" We have invited Mrs. Gavin, the math teacher, who also played *Pomp and Circumstance* for each graduation's senior procession, and "Hand Grenade Hank" Doyle, whom I thanked profusely at our thirty-fifth reunion for his pastoral care of me. I always drive by the three houses I lived in, all standing; the empty field where the cow barn was; and the house that once was the shul, so central to my boyhood. Finally, there is my red brick school, for all twelve grades, now administrative offices of the "system," with newer classroom buildings in a campus surround. The nostalgic trip through boyhood always ends with Miriam's pronouncement: "This is the last time."

Sigmund entered my life because of Miriam. She had an older brother, with whom she was quite close, and she decided that if I had a brother living in Peabody, we should get to know him. So we did and fell in love with him and his family. He and his Helen lived in a picture-book suburban house that was immaculately clean and full of adorable domestic knickknacks like creamers shaped like cows. Ziggy, as we came to call him, was somewhat reserved, but friendly, with a lovely smile. Helen, on the other hand, was bubbly, warm, and cuddly. She came from a fairly large, tight-knit Greek family presided over by patriarchal Socko and was thrilled that her Ziggy now had a family. We were, too, as we were immediately accepted by her

Fig. 15 |
Sigmund
Kramnick, Isaac's
older brother

extended family as close kin. I, too, had found family, a warm and loving family, my family. Ziggy's conversion to Greek Orthodoxy had enabled them to adopt a little boy and then a little girl, and we were honored guests at their christenings and at fabulous Greek holiday dinners. In the 1960s they were a focus of our social life.

On visits to Peabody we sometimes saw my father, by then a recluse living in the same third-floor apartment in Little's Lane, with newspapers on top of tables and dressers. Max retained his faculties but seemed a stranger to me, smiling, seemingly lost in his own world. I asked both him and Ziggy for pictures of my mother, Sarah, and to my amazement, neither had any. I got the sense it was a kind of folk response to mental illness: throw away pictures and you banish the curse. Not until my files from the state arrived in 1979 did I learn what my mother looked like. When Max died, Ziggy took care of everything. I didn't go to the funeral.

There was much to catch up on with Ziggy in those years. He didn't have much to say about growing up with Sarah, Max, and Leon, and then with Max. What little he remembered focused on his trumpet and the high school band. He told me of Korea, the GI Bill, and studying journalism at Boston University. His first job was in charge of publications for the National Fire Protection Association in Boston, but since he wanted to do real journalism, he took a job as a reporter for the *New Britain Herald*, in Connecticut, writing obituaries and short stories. Helen missed Peabody, so Ziggy went back, working for Hoods Milk, the largest milk and ice cream company in the Boston area, famous for its little ice cream cups called "hoodsies." His job was editing the internal publication that went to all of Hood's employees, suppliers, and distributors.

From there he moved up to a job at the John Hancock Life Insurance Company, which is when Ziggy entered my life, bringing such joy to me, this quiet man of words, working his way up the corporate ladder. About a year after Ziggy entered my life, Leon did, too, suddenly and through no initiative of mine. On a Friday morning in the spring of 1964, the bell rang in our apartment at the Harvard married graduate student residence hall on Irving Street in Cambridge. At the door I saw a chubby, disheveled, and dirty middle-aged, round-faced man, smiling. He introduced himself as my brother Leon; he had been given my address by Ziggy, he announced loudly. Obviously high-strung, he talked rapidly or whistled, though he seemed a surprisingly gentle big man. I was struck by his huge fingernails. We were heading off for a weekend trip but invited him to stay in the apartment while we were gone, suggesting that he could use our bath and listen to some of our records. Thus began our well-meaning, naïve effort to rehabilitate Leon.

We called Ziggy that night, who apologized for not having warned us about Leon, an "oversight" I probably rooted in the embarrassment evoked by the thought or mention of him. Ziggy now filled us in. Two years ago, Ziggy reported, Leon, having been in Danvers State Hospital for over twenty years, during which time he had had several regimens of electroshock therapy, was discharged as part of the movement of deinstitutionalization and "mainstreaming" in family- or community-based mental health care. He'd come to live at 3 Little's Lane, where he resumed his stormy relationship with Max, who, unlike Sigmund, had continued to visit him at Danvers. Leon got a job selling newspaper subscriptions over the phone, but he'd often lose his temper with a prospect and after a few months lost his job. Fighting constantly with Max, he left Little's Lane and took to the streets, becoming part of the army of homeless mentally ill, eating trash, sleeping in doorways or subways, occasionally getting jobs washing dishes, though, as he told us, such work was becoming hard to find if you weren't Hispanic. Sometimes he panhandled as a street performer—a whistler. He went back and forth between Boston and New York, and a return to Boston precipitated the visit to us.

Miriam and I returned from our weekend convinced that if we connected Leon with the right social agency, he would be set on the path to normalcy through work and therapy. Ziggy dismissed the plan with tales of efforts to help, all of which ended with him giving Leon money. Meanwhile, when we tried to talk with Leon about his boyhood or about Danvers, all he would say is that both Max and the hospital staff mistreated him and that only our mother Sarah, whom he said I looked like, loved him. He preferred to talk of life on the street.

Sure enough, as we gamely scouted social service agencies, Leon hit the road, leaving Boston for New York. For years he would enter our lives at unexpected times, in unexpected ways. Two or three times a year in the late 1960s and through the 1970s I got phone calls from exotic places, once a prison in Milwaukee that was giving vagrants a Christmas release, once from the traveler's aid desk at New York's Port Authority Bus Terminal, and once from Bellevue Hospital. The message was always a variation of "There's a man here named Leon Kramnick who needs money and says you are his brother and will wire him cash." Leon sensed I was a softer touch than Ziggy, and, of course, I dutifully headed off to Western Union and sent $50 to a man who could answer "Sarah Sushelsky" to the question "What is your mother's maiden name?"

In the early 1970s, when I taught at Yale, Leon sometimes called to ask if he could visit. I decided, callously and like a coward, that I didn't want him in our house in North Haven's assistant professor ghetto, nor did I want to explain him to our children. Most of all I trembled at the possibility that he might disrupt my Yale classes. So I always arranged to meet him at New Haven's Greyhound terminal, where I bought him dinner, gave him money, and sent him on his way, which may well have been all he wanted anyway.

When we moved to Ithaca, the calls from Leon diminished, though I never stopped worrying about him showing up unexpectedly. I avoided him that sunny day on Fifth Avenue in 1975, and the last phone call for money came in 1979. After a while I assumed that he had died on a street somewhere, perhaps killed in a street brawl, an unknown with no identification and no information about a person to notify "in case of emergency." So disappeared from my life my oldest brother, whom I met when I was twenty-six, and who lived such a tragic life: a deeply troubled childhood, decades in a mental hospital, decades living on the street. No American dream here—born in Poland, an anonymous death in anywhere, USA.

Moving to Ithaca meant seeing less of Ziggy and Helen, our new family, but we kept up by frequent long phone calls. So it was in the late summer of 1973 that we were not surprised to get a call from Helen, which quickly turned to horror. Through her tearful sobs we learned that she and a friend had taken their children to Cape Cod on a two-week vacation, to be joined by their husbands on the weekends. Ziggy never came. He had sat in their car in their Peabody garage, turned on the ignition, and asphyxiated himself.

We drove immediately to Peabody, unable to comprehend the suicidal ending of what seemed such a happy and successful life. Through the wailing of the funeral and the several days that followed we heard tales of corporate tension, a failed promotion, someone else getting the job Ziggy expected to get at John Hancock. In the months and years that followed we heard stories suggesting that behind the picture-book house and marriage, Ziggy was a problematic father, a rigid disciplinarian. Tensions in the marriage were created by Helen serving as a social brake on Ziggy's ambitions, her reluctance to entertain or go to parties generated by feelings of inadequacy as a non–college graduate. Whatever the explanation, the paradox remains: the brother whose boyhood was the closest to ordinary, with a continuous household (albeit somewhat dysfunctional), the one brother who had a modicum of psychic stability, killed himself at the age of forty-three. No American dream here, either.

But this was not the last of the strange twists and turns in the story of the Brothers K. Leon had, in fact, not died. In 2001, my son, by then a college professor, sent me an e-mail one day in January that he would call at eight that evening and that I should have a scotch in hand and be seated when I took the call. I followed both instructions, and he told me that while he had been googling himself, he had come across a *Hartford Courant* newspaper columnist's story of April 1997 with the opening line, "Leon Kramnick, perhaps the most recognized person in downtown Hartford, died last week of a heart attack, at 73. I celebrate him."

In the late 1970s Leon had befriended several Christian evangelists who had a literature table inside the then notoriously seedy Manhattan Port Authority Bus Terminal. With their help over several months he pledged himself to Christ and, cleaned up and openly devout, joined their Christian community in New Rochelle, New York. In the early 1980s, he lived with the group with occasional forays back to the streets. In January 1982 he went with one of the community's founders—who had been chosen to head the Church of the Risen Savior—to South Windsor, Connecticut, near Hartford. In South Windsor he lived in a comfortable Victorian house as part of the minister's extended family, his wife and three children, and several other lost souls, lovingly incorporated into the Christian home. Almost every weekday for fifteen years Leon took the bus to downtown Hartford, where for part of the day he recited poetry, sang, or chanted on street corners. He became a familiar figure to the daytime crowds, many of whom worked in the city's insurance company home offices. They called him "the poet," and with his round cherubic face and full white beard, he was said to look like a bard of old.

People knew he was in some way mentally ill; he indeed called himself "king of the loonies" and sometimes urged passersby to "take a crazy person to lunch." He might scream at passing airplanes, but his decent clothes, gentleness, and evident piety won people over, and for years he was a colorful folk hero in downtown Hartford. At noon almost every day he could be found at the Catholic bookstore, ecumenically sharing in midday mass. He befriended there a widowed vice president of Traveler's Insurance, who became a sometime companion for concerts and plays. In the evenings he returned to his adopted home surrounded by Christian love. Leon never contacted me during his Hartford years and apparently did not tell his Christian family about his professor brother. He had fifteen years of contentment and love in Connecticut, his death in 1997 marked with the elegiac article by Tom Condon in the *Hartford Courant*, "The Curtain Closes for a Poet Who Spoke His Vision."

Miriam and I tracked down Leon's South Windsor family, Ben and Liz Torrey, and visited them in the fall of 2001. We visited Leon's grave, and then over dinner in their home, we heard stories of Leon's fascination with music, old movies, and the Red Sox. It seems he could hear a piece of classical music and, more often than not, identify the composer, even if he had not heard the particular piece before. We were shown photos of him over the years, especially at Christmas dinners, surrounded by adoring Torrey children. With his beard, tweed jacket, and Tattersall shirt, he looked the very model of an aging English professor. The Torreys gave us a shoebox full of Leon's poetry, most written on the backs of envelopes, singling out their favorite, the one Condon had quoted in his newspaper celebration of Leon: "I Am the Lost," a Whitmanesque poem about street life as Leon knew it.

I am the Lost
I am 1,000 scoldings, I am 1,000 no-nos,
I am 10,000 lonely beds of tears. I am demented,
I am dead of life,
I am the one living in the gutter. I am the one in Hartford Hotel.
I am the one waiting in line at the out-patient,
I am every patient in Norwich, Middletown, Elmcrest. I need
    you brother.
I speak for all my lost. I need the Lord,
I am the one he came for. I am the lowly
I am the eternal schizo.
I am the derelict with no name. I am the one who can't get in. I
    am the shunned.
I am a thousand diagnoses.
I séance through a 1,000 psycho-therapy sessions.

I am the years, the voyages through a thousand traumas. I died
with Him,
Rose from death and am alive.

Leon in the end had made something of himself. He tamed his
street self, his wayward self, reserving it for weekday hours peppered
with poetry. And his life ended with years of evening joy and love.
My sad and tragic reading of his end was wrong. This new sense
of Leon in his latter days complicates somewhat the symmetry of
the Brothers K with the findings of research about the children of
schizophrenics, like Sarah. Studies show that they tend by and large
to be self-destructive, dysfunctional, or creative. Ziggy was certainly
self-destructive; I seem to be the creative one, and Leon, the puta-
tive dysfunctional, had, it turns out, a strong creative bent, as, of
course, did Ziggy.

If I am the creative brother predicted in the scholarly literature,
I have, as I have already noted, by no means been left unscarred by
my childhood; I have my demi-demons. Hardly a week goes by without dreams involving abandonment and loss or of love suddenly and
inexplicably terminated. I easily distrust others and I have a Saul-
like tendency to mock the pretentious and self-assured. I have never
overcome the fear of being exposed as a fraud, apparently often a
characteristic of first-generation professionals, though sometimes
I too proudly see my life as incomparable, a unique story of success and achievement that leaves me stupidly intolerant of other
people's tales of childhood pain. I am an incessant worrier, my children tell me, and religion, alas, offers no solace. I have abandoned
all boyhood beliefs and practices, though I am still proud to be an
American Jew.

For some creative people, work can prove to be a way of working
through personal psychic issues and expressing a sense of self. In my
case, my first two books explored the ideas of the eighteenth-century conservative thinkers Bolingbroke and Burke, emphasizing
their normative ideals of roots, continuity, and tradition. Was I
drawn to them from my own quest for roots, a "state kid" with
no family, no continuity, no connections? Was I drawn to them
also as a middle- to late-twentieth-century American Jew, with no

experience of roots or family continuity beyond the grandparents' generation? Alongside the analysis in my work on the defense of privilege and of men "to the manor born" is a contradictory interest in the "self-made" man as the fundamental ideal in American political thought. From Benjamin Franklin through Abraham Lincoln unto Barack Obama, the American dream requires self-creation in a mythic world of equal opportunity, where anyone with talent and merit can win in the race of life. I teach my students that this is a mythic ideal, and that for every Franklin, Lincoln, and Obama, for every John D. Rockefeller, Andrew Carnegie, and Bill Gates, there are legions more who never realize the American dream. What I haven't shared with my students, even as I shatter the myth, is that I am myself this paradigmatic self-created, self-made, successful man who embodies America's mythic ideal, the American dream, and that I am fiercely proud of it. I share it with them now.

There is, finally, one last surprising twist in this rapid summary of my not-that-atypical story after college. My foster mother, Helen, that Dickensian character in my Dickensian boyhood, was well and active until she died in 2012 at the age of 105. After Saul died, she led an independent existence, driving, shopping, and cooking for herself well into her nineties. Amazingly healthy and energetic, she continued her intense involvement with Hadassah, trooping off to meetings. She had not mellowed much in her old age, remaining self-centered, penny-pinching, and unaffectionate. In her mid-nineties she moved to a kosher Jewish continuous care community in Chelsea, at the foot of the Tobin Bridge. We visited her there and celebrated her birthdays as the community's oldest resident. She was, as they say in Massachusetts, still "shahp as a tack," with childhood memories on easy recall, when she wasn't grumbling about how the assisted living's Shabbos services had been shortened too much and how the returns on her modest investments were too little. Such, then, is the ironic end of my story. I, who as a boy never knew my mother, had, unlike anyone my age, a mother still—fifty years after case #24269, "Isaac Kramnick, Village Street, Millis," was closed, and I was "discharged to self."